JONAS BROTHERS

Inside Their World

THERS

Inside Their World

Brittany Kent

BERKLEY BOULEVARD BOOKS, NEW YORK

INTERIOR PHOTOS:

MARK ASHMAN:
pages 31, 32, 83, 102–103, 104, 124, 157, 163, 168

JOE MAGNANI:
pages ii, x, 21, 22, 23, 24, 38, 40, 42, 43, 62, 74, 75, 77, 80, 81, 86, 87, 92, 93, 105, 106, 107, 108, 109, 110, 111, 113, 114, 115, 116, 118, 119, 121, 122–123, 127, 129, 130, 133, 134, 135, 136, 140, 143, 144, 145, 146, 147, 151, 154, 156, 161, 165, 166, 175, 182

THE BERKLEY PUBLISHING GROUP
Published by the Penguin Group
Penguin Group (USA) Inc.
375 Hudson Street, New York, New York 10014, USA
Penguin Group (Canada), 90 Eglinton Avenue East, Suite 700, Toronto, Ontario M4P 2Y3, Canada
(a division of Pearson Penguin Canada Inc.)
Penguin Books Ltd., 80 Strand, London WC2R 0RL, England
Penguin Group Ireland, 25 St. Stephen's Green, Dublin 2, Ireland (a division of Penguin Books Ltd.)
Penguin Group (Australia), 250 Camberwell Road, Camberwell, Victoria 3124, Australia
(a division of Pearson Australia Group Pty. Ltd.)
Penguin Books India Pvt. Ltd., 11 Community Centre, Panchsheel Park, New Delhi—110 017, India
Penguin Group (NZ), 67 Apollo Drive, Rosedale, North Shore 0632, New Zealand
(a division of Pearson New Zealand Ltd.)
Penguin Books (South Africa) (Pty.) Ltd., 24 Sturdee Avenue, Rosebank, Johannesburg 2196,
South Africa

Penguin Books Ltd., Registered Offices: 80 Strand, London WC2R 0RL, England

The publisher does not have any control over and does not assume any responsibility for author or third-party websites or their content.

JONAS BROTHERS: INSIDE THEIR WORLD

Printing History
Berkley Boulevard trade paperback edition / June 2009

ISBN: 978-0-425-22939-2

PRINTED IN THE UNITED STATES OF AMERICA

10 9 8 7 6 5 4 3 2 1

contents

Over the past few years, the world has been amazed by the rise to fame of a band of three brothers named Nick, Joe, and Kevin. The Jonas Brothers started their careers rocking out in churches and at state fairs, inspired by their musical parents and supported by the faith they had in their abilities. They were not an overnight success, but it was still dazzling when they hit the big time, conquering radio with hit singles, the Internet with hilarious YouTube videos, and arenas all over the planet with their sold-out live shows. For once, the good guys had won—and won big!

I'm a huge Jonas fan. I love seeing new bands, and I just about died when I caught them at B.B. King's in Manhattan in 2006. They were so polished, such pros onstage, so full of energy as they presented their undeniably catchy songs. Like many of you, I was hooked the first time I saw and heard these charming boys.

There's something special about loving the Jonas Brothers because what really blows us away isn't just how cute they are, but also how devoted they are to their music, and what genuinely good guys they are. They appreciate their fans, thanking them at every turn, and they are extremely humble about the rock star position in which they find themselves.

Part of why they're all so grounded has to do with the motto their father gave them—"Live like you're still at the bottom." To remember that, Kevin started saying "Living the dream!" after all their shows. They never want to forget that every single thing they get to do in their lives and careers is a blessing.

I know I speak for all their fans out there when I say that we feel the same way—we appreciate every new record or video or live performance they give us! I'm writing this book as a Valentine to the Jonas Brothers, but also to you guys, the fans, because only we truly understand how much these boys mean to us.

I sincerely hope you'll love this book as much as I've loved writing it!

xoxo Brittany Kent

how the JoBros made it!

As you might suspect from their love of music, the Jonas Brothers come from musical parents. And their parents didn't just pass on their musical talents—they also passed on to their children love, faith, and humility, traits the boys carry to this day.

Paul Kevin Jonas from North Carolina and Denise Miller from Arizona first met at the Christ for the Nations Bible College in Dallas. In addition to sharing a strong Christian faith—they were devoted enough to their religion to consider going on missions around the world—Kevin (who never went by "Paul") was a singer gifted with the ability to play several instruments, and Denise was a talented vocalist in her own right.

On August 15, 1985—within a year of meeting—the couple were wed. Kevin was twenty-one and Denise just nineteen, but they were madly in love and had felt in sync from the first time they'd met. After marriage, Denise taught sign language and Kevin became a pastor, a job that allowed him to support his family while still devoting his life to God.

On November 5, 1987, while in Teaneck, New Jersey, the young couple joyfully welcomed their first son into the world, naming him Paul Kevin Jonas II—though, just like his dad, he would always go by Kevin. Their second son, Joseph Adam Jonas, arrived on their fourth anniversary in 1989 while they were staying with Denise's family in Casa Grande, Arizona; and their third child, Nicholas Jerry Jonas, was born on September 16, 1992, back in Dallas, Texas.

"Our parents were ministers and they went everywhere," Kevin told *Bop* in March 2008. "I was born in New Jersey, then we moved to Arizona because my dad wanted to try songwriting. That's where Joe was born, but it didn't work out there, so we moved to Texas, where Nick was born."

By this point, Kevin Sr. had taken a job at his old alma mater, Christ for the Nations, in Dallas and Denise found work in the registrar's office. Both sang in Christian music groups, and they were frequently on the road pursuing their pastime. "Their crib was in the back of a van, we would set up a little play area in the back when Kevin was little, and Joseph's first car seat was literally the strongbox where we kept the finances," Denise told *People*.

As a baby, Kevin was "the talkative one," his dad told *People*, though he also revealed that Kevin used to lisp. Joe, however, was Kevin's polar opposite. "He was always kind of quiet," Denise recalled. According to Kevin Sr., Joe was "very mellow from birth, like the opposite of what he is now. Then when he was in the second or third grade, he started to come out of his shell, and he never went back. More than anybody else, when he hit the stage, he surprised us."

"Kevin talked a lot when we were kids, almost *too much*," Joe ratted to *Life Story*. "It was my birthday one time—and we have videotape proof of this—and we're all having fun. I'm a smiley baby, and the door swings open and it's Kevin. His curly head is by the door and he's screaming out, 'It's my birthday party!' They said it was *my* birthday party and he started to cry. It was like, 'Who invited this guy?' It was a Barney birthday party, by the way." Despite this documented act of big-brotherly terrorism, the guys rarely fought and considered themselves to be each other's best friends in the world.

homes sweet homes

In 2007, there was controversy among JoBros fans over rumors that the guys had officially moved to the West Coast. Fans liked the idea of them staying in New Jersey, but the fact is that the guys have always moved around (New Jersey, Texas, Arizona), so relocating to California was just another example of their wandering ways! Kevin told *Life Story*, "I can't believe how much we love California. We have amazing friends out there now, and that's where we consider our 'base.'"

In 2008, the Jonas Brothers expanded their collection of residences, buying a mansion in Westlake, Texas. "It's just like a random place to go on vacation. It doesn't even feel real. I get in a golf cart, go straight to the course. They're like, 'Hey, Mr. Jonas, you going to play today?' It's the best thing *ever*," Kevin said to *Rolling Stone*.

"Being the baby, I got away with everything," Nick admitted to *Twist* in its October/November 2006 issue. As a toddler, "Nick figured out he could open the cabinets. He used to climb in the cabinet, unscrew the top to this glass container and eat all of the pretzels. I'd walk in and he would just smile at me," Denise Jonas recalled in the May/June 2008 issue of *J-14*. But Nick was as serious as a baby as he is now. "He was always thinking with such intensity he would wrinkle his forehead," Kevin Sr. remembered. Nick was also a curious child who loved toys that played music—foreshadowing his eventual career. The first song he ever sang, he has said, was probably something from *Peter Pan*.

As they grew, all three were just like any normal boys their ages—they were noisy, messy, and rambunctious and loved to play cowboys and Indians (Kevin told *Twist* in October 2006, "Joe was always the one being hunted down!"), even if they were ultimately very well-behaved and goal-oriented kids.

The Jonas family always had a trampoline in their backyard and all three brothers loved to make movies of themselves jumping on it.

"Growing up, we didn't really play pranks on each other, but we put Gak in one of my dad's dress shoes," Kevin said to *J-14* in April 2008. "He was going to work, and it was all [making squishing noises]. We were never allowed to have Gak, Floam, or any of that stuff in the house ever again."

Their home life was idyllic, with attentive mom Denise home at all times to watch over them. "My mom likes to cook for us because she's been made to cook," Nick told *Tiger Beat Celebrity Spectacular!* in Fall 2008. "It's like, 'I need to cook for you. Don't touch anything. Sit down. Let me take care of you.'" Their fave dish? Her sweet-potato casserole!

Nick told *Tiger Beat* in June 2008, "[Jonas family dinners] are big with us. We've done that our whole life. We talk about normal stuff." Joe described the family dinners as "awesome—a lot of laughing and talking. Our house is definitely a loud house. We have a lot of family friends who come a lot."

Easter is a major holiday in the Jonas household—when they were little, the boys would have to search for their baskets based on how old they were. Nick's basket would be hidden somewhere on one floor of the house, while older brothers Kevin and Joe had to search three floors for theirs. Nick said their mom "cooks a wonderful Easter dinner. Every year, there is something weird in the shape of a lamb on our supper table—like a mound of butter or a cake." But when it comes to dyeing eggs, Kevin told *J-14* in April 2006, "Every year we destroy our kitchen." Their most eventful Easter came when a well-off family they were friends with hosted an Easter egg hunt in their sprawling backyard. "They had eggs full of money—no candy, just money," Kevin remembered. "There were eggs with $50, with 10 cents and pennies. You had to run and shake the egg. And if it jingled, you'd move on to another egg. It got brutal!"

What were the guys like as they got older?

Kevin was the studious type, already a concerned citizen at a young age—he even ran for student council! He wore glasses and was "the geeky kid," Denise told *J-14*'s May/June 2008 issue, "but he was friendly and outgoing." He loved having a bike rack connected to the ceiling of his room in Dallas—he could hoist his bicycle up and attach it to the contraption, keeping it inside and near him at all times. His best friend at the time was a boy named Zack—the two of them considered themselves the leaders of all the neighborhood boys, in the same way that Kevin felt he was leader of the pack among his bros.

Joe was shy, and occasionally got teased in grade school. But little did his parents realize, he'd concocted a whole different identity for himself at school! According to the May/June 2008 issue of *J-14*, his parents didn't find out about this until they had a conference with his teacher, who kept calling him "J.J." When they tried to explain that they were Joseph Jonas's parents, the teacher looked at them funny, and said, "Yeah, J.J." "We just laughed because [we'd] never heard that name for him!" Ironically, though, Joe didn't like his "J.J." nickname. "Kids would call me J.J. They'd go, 'J.J. Jonas!' I hated it."

One time, when Joe was feeling kind of down over something that he'd been teased about, Nick and Kevin cheered him up by repeatedly saying, "Look at you!" When he looked in the mirror, he realized what a mistake it was to be sad when everything in his life was going so right. "I hugged these guys and gave them a kiss on the cheek. These are my brothers. I love them." What a close-knit clan!

How close are they? "We give each other looks all the time where only we know what it means," Nick told *Bop* in November 2007. Their "secret language of the JoBros" meant the guys could have entire conversations that would completely befuddle anyone happening to listen in.

Overall, the boys' early years in Texas were charmed, though not without a few scrapes.

"I remember one time when everyone was like, 'Where's Nick? Where's Nick?'" Joe told *Life Story*. "He'd snuck over the fence and jumped into the pool and he was really young. Too young to be swimming in a pool, which was *really* scary."

Then there was the time when Kevin Sr. was teaching Kevin how to pump gas. "The spray got in my eyes! I freaked out and ran screaming to the bathroom in the gas station. I remember knocking things over!" Kevin recalled in Summer 2008's *Tiger Beat Celebrity Spectacular!*

Joe also used to love throwing apples from their yard out into the woods to hear them go *splat* against the trees. Once, a bee was on the apple, and even though Joe hurried to get rid of it, the bee hung around and stung him on the hand. He's never forgotten it.

But the most serious incident occurred during one of their long car trips to visit relatives, when the family got into a huge car accident. "We did a lot of driving during our summer vacations," Kevin remembered. "The typical drive was always hot and we would be passed out in the backseat." They often went to visit their mom's family in Arizona. "We spent a lot of summers in Arizona hanging out at a local skateboard shop where my uncle worked," Kevin told *Bop* in May 2008. "That's where I learned how to skate." But in this instance, the accident occurred during one of their long car trips to South Carolina to visit Kevin Sr.'s family. "Joe and Nick were asleep," Kevin remembered to *Tiger Beat* in September 2006. "It was 8 a.m. and Joe put his glasses on to see this truck coming toward us

DID YOU KNOW? The guys almost named themselves Sons of Jonas before settling on The Jonas Brothers!

from behind—vrooooooooom. We all woke up at that exact moment. We got hit by an 18-wheeler truck." The driver had fallen asleep at the wheel. When the truck hit the Jonases' car, it shattered the windows, sending glass everywhere. Joe had tucked Nick under his arm to protect him. "The guy who hit us walks up out of the truck and goes, 'Everybody all right?' We were like, 'Are you kidding me? You just hit us with a Mack truck!'" They were very, very lucky, however—everyone was okay. Kevin felt that the impact might've been partially absorbed by all their luggage in the back, possibly saving them from serious injury or even worse!

In 1996, the Jonases—struggling financially—moved across the country to the city of Wyckoff in Bergen County, New Jersey, following a new job that had opened up for Kevin as the pastor of an Assembly of God church. The move was hard on the boys. "We've had to switch schools," Joe commiserated with a distressed fan who was going through a move in *m* magazine in May 2007. "IM or phone calls help with keeping in touch. Try to plan trips once in a while so that you can get back to see your friends."

In Wyckoff, the Jonases lived in the gray parsonage right next to their father's church. "The church was a wonderful place," Kevin recalled in *Life Story*. "It has a stage—an awesome stage with a full drum set and platforms. It was full of music all the time, and that's where we learned about performing and singing." The boys remember their mother's voice as "beautiful" when she accompanied them and their dad.

"We grew up in church, playing with our father onstage," Kevin told *Rolling Stone*. Kevin and Joe's greatest moment in church was probably singing "I Am Amazed," a sweet hymn penned by their father—footage of that adorably awkward debut continues to attract crazy numbers of views on YouTube.

The guys continued getting along great in their new home, supporting each other and meshing well. "When I was 14, Kevin was at the age that he wanted to hang out with girls and Nick was of the age that he liked to go and get ice cream. I was right in the middle and I liked ice cream *and* I liked girls, so it worked out well," Joe told *Life Story*.

Kevin Sr.'s new position had a larger congregation and

immediately took up even more of his time. He was on call constantly and worked every day until very late at night. This made it difficult for the boys to be involved in sports leagues and other extracurricular activities, since Kevin Sr. had to be at work even on the weekends.

So instead of school programs, the Jonases played in a local playground, which had a soccer field and tennis courts. It was a wealthy area, but the family's income was still very modest, so the guys had to entertain themselves on a budget. Joe loved the Nature Center, a beautiful area filled with flora and fauna that was just a couple of blocks from their home. "I'd go to the Nature Center every morning and go running," Joe told *Life Story*. "I'd see deer roaming around. It was so quiet and peaceful."

Kevin told *Tiger Beat* in December 2007 that the coolest place in town was Boulder Run. "It's where my friends and I get together." This popular, open-air minimall features a Starbucks next to a McDonald's next to a Blockbuster, a killer candy shop, and a CD store—all in a row. "It's like all your needs in one place!" Kevin told *Tiger Beat* in December 2006.

In the summers, they were close enough to the beach to enjoy weekends at the Jersey Shore, and in the winter, they had the added benefit of being able to build snow forts in the backyard. Kevin told *J-14* in January 2008, "My favorite memory ever was the year it snowed so much in New Jersey that we only had three days of school in a week. I built a pretty amazing igloo in my backyard. We filled big, square Tupperware containers with snow, packed them down, and flipped them over like bricks."

Speed demon Joe preferred the sledding. "In New

best and worst parts of being in a brother band?

The best part? "You can look across the stage and know you have a support system that is rock solid," the guys told *Twist* in July 2006 when asked for the best part of being in a band of brothers. The worst part? "You look across the stage and your brothers are still there!" Good one, guys!

Ultimately, the boys are happy together because, as Kevin later said in the same issue, "We make each other better!"

"You have a security that everything is going to be okay, even when you mess up," Kevin said in 2006 while the guys were making their first *Total Request Live* appearance with JoJo, the platinum-selling singer whose songs "Leave (Get Out)" and "Baby It's You" helped make her a household name.

Jersey, they have some crazy hills for sledding. They're crazy dangerous! A few times, I actually went down hills and tripped somebody, like you see in the movies. Sledding was the best!" Joe told *J-14* in January 2008.

Nick told the same magazine about his memories of the snow days: "I was eight . . . Both of my best friends were off from school, and we played this game outside where we lived an imaginary life [called Snow Mountain]. I think I got frostbite, but it's all good."

Still, the best and cheapest way to busy themselves was with music, and their father encouraged his boys to express what he saw as their God-given talents. Music filled the Jonas household at all times. Kevin Sr. loved Stevie Wonder, James Taylor, Carole King, and—throughout the '90s—pop producers such as Max Martin (Backstreet Boys, Britney Spears). "We'd have friends over and we'd be listening to the new Backstreet Boys CD, and he'd talk about how amazing Max Martin was," Nick told *Rolling Stone.* "Dad's always taken the *Billboard* chart and dissected it."

"Our father is an amazing musician and singer," Kevin told *Life Story* in Winter 2008. "He's the kind of person who can pick up any instrument, and within a few minutes he'll be playing a tune on it. At the church, where our father was pastor, there was always music and singing, and I spent years on the stage there with my dad. That's where we all started singing and playing."

That musicality was not totally appreciated *all* of the time. "When Joe was younger, he would always get really, really embarrassed by my dad," Nick revealed to *J-14* in April 2008. "When we would eat at Johnny Rockets, where they play old-time music, my dad would get up and start singing all the songs. I thought it was awesome. I didn't really care; I would sing with him. But Joe used to get so embarrassed!"

Copying his dad at home, Nick would sing show tunes from on top of the family's coffee table, using a turkey baster as his mic. When sternly told to get down, he reportedly said, "No, Mama. I need to practice. I'm gonna be on Broadway."

Nick told *People*, "I'd make my own tickets out of construction paper and sell them for $5." He'd often mimic

*NSYNC and the Backstreet Boys, using his built-in backups—his brothers—to flesh out his act. At one of their earliest public performances together, the guys performed a Backstreet Boys song at a local wedding.

Kevin, too, was bitten by the music bug. He knew he wanted to perform as soon as he saw a pal do it. "I saw a friend of mine performing and I knew I wanted to be in a band," he told *People*. "I asked to be in a bunch of bands in high school, but no one would have me."

He finally taught himself how to play the guitar using a *Teach Yourself Guitar* book. He told *Fans' Choice: Triple Treat!* in December 2007, "I was home sick one day and I didn't want to watch *Dora the Explorer* anymore or *Blue's Clue*s on Nickelodeon because that was the only thing on in the morning. I turned off the TV and picked up the book and I just read it and picked up a guitar and just chord by chord I went."

Living in New Jersey held the value of being close to Manhattan, the perfect place for a family whose sons were beginning to explore their creativity—and a city that would soon play a huge role in the boys' lives and careers. "New York City was a dream city for us," Kevin said in *Life Story*. "It's not so far from New Jersey, but it's a whole other, magical place. There's nothing like it, and we got to go quite often, which was a joy for us."

"My wife and I never imagined we were raising children who would become famous performers," Kevin Sr. told *Life Story* in Winter 2008. "We were raising our sons to become good people, good men, and that's what makes us proudest of them, that they've become such wonderful people."

Kevin thinks his parents allowed the guys to pursue their dreams out of hope, not ambition. "They saw something more in their kids—in a humble manner—that said, possibly it was something that could work."

The first Jonas to connect in the entertainment industry professionally was the (then) youngest—Nick used to go with his mom to the hair salon, where he would perform spontaneously in exchange for candy and pennies. He was noticed by a woman whose child had starred on Broadway. She strongly encouraged Denise to find Nick a manager immediately, telling her that Nick looked and sounded as capable as her own child, who was already a success story.

Nick proved to be excellent in auditions, singing and acting with confidence despite having little training. He would go on to star in Broadway productions of *A Christmas Carol: The Musical*, *Annie Get Your Gun*, *Beauty and the Beast* ("I played Chip the teacup in *Beauty and the Beast*," Nick told *Twist* in September 2006; "it was my favorite play to be in"), and *Les Misérables* (playing urchin Gavroche). Nick thoroughly enjoyed these experiences—he said he loved performing more than he loved toys!—feeling like he was discovering what he was going to do with the rest of his life.

"Broadway was amazing—I loved it!" Nick told *Popstar!* in May 2008. "I feel like it was really good training for what I'm doing now. It was more *fun* than a job. I always hated it when people would be like, 'Oh, I have to go to work today,' and they'd be living their dream. You lose sight of what's actually going on and how amazing an opportunity it is!"

Still, while he was understudying the role of Tiny Tim in *A Christmas Carol* on Broadway, Nick had the ultimate embarrassing moment for a performer—he froze up! "They had an emergency rehearsal for an hour," Nick told *J-14* in December 2007. "I got on the stage, and the conductor was the scariest guy I had ever seen. I couldn't sing—nothing came out!"

But that setback aside, Nick loved Broadway for teaching him how to act, a skill that comes in handy to this day, considering the high drama involved in staging a rock concert. Although rock concerts sound like more work than musicals! "On Broadway, you don't have to work the crowd and get them hyped up," Nick explained to *Life Story* in Winter 2008. "It's more about just your character connecting with them, as well as the music and the story itself."

Nick told *Rolling Stone* in its October 30, 2008, issue that his Broadway success snuck up on him. "A kid, a family friend, came up and asked for an autograph, and I was like, 'You're my friend! Why are you asking me for my autograph?'"

During this period, the guys attended Eastern Christian Middle School at 518 Sicomac Avenue in Wyckoff, New Jersey. The school was very helpful toward the Jonases when it came to being flexible about their schedules (they repaid the debt with a free concert in the 505-seat auditorium when they became famous), and so Nick stayed in regular school except for Wednesdays (matinee days!) and learned how to play the drums in church bands.

Later, when homeschooling became a must, Nick took to writing reviews of TV shows, albums, and movies for creative-writing extra credit to supplement his schoolwork.

While the family drove their little Broadway star to and from rehearsals and performances, the brothers would all hone their songwriting skills. Joe and Kevin were inspired by Nick's path, so it wasn't long before all three boys were signed to management deals. This led to Kevin and Joe starting out in commercials. They plugged products for Office Depot, Clorox, and Burger King (funny that the Jonas Brothers would later be signed to an endorsement deal by the fast-food chain!)

Denise managed to take her sons to multiple auditions in spite of being pregnant with her fourth child. Those auditions were at least as nerve-wracking for Denise as they were for the boys!

"I really observed the other parents," Denise told *Rolling Stone*. "I thought, 'I'm a novice, and I don't want to make any mistakes that could be detrimental to us as a family or their careers down the road.' We weighed *everything*. Sometimes they'd throw a script at us that was full of language not suitable for a seven-year-old."

The Jonases felt pressured sometimes by other parents, who would imply showbiz could be destructive to solid morals, but open-minded Kevin Sr. felt the plays his kids starred in were "beautiful works of art." Besides, to offset any concerns about their spirituality, the boys remained very active in their church.

Joe even went on a mission to Mexico at age eleven.

In the middle of all this excitement, on September 28, 2000, the final Jonas sibling was born—Franklin Nathaniel Jonas came as a surprise eight years after Nick, and he never stopped surprising the family with his mischievous sense of humor and independent streak.

"I love being the mother of all boys," Denise told *m* in May 2007. "They're different, but they complement each other so well!"

Meanwhile, although Joe liked acting—he'd even landed the part of the Artful Dodger in a local production of the musical *Oliver!* (Nick landed the lead, but had to bow out in favor of a Broadway show)—he was very against the idea of singing. "I did *not* want to sing!" Joe told *Popstar!* in July 2006. "I just wanted to be on *All That*—that was *my* show. Especially with Kenan Thompson and Kel Mitchell back in the day. I would *love* to bring back *All That*!" Joe especially hated opera. Yet he was next in line for a New York City stage debut, in Baz Luhrmann's 2002 production of the opera *La Bohème.* Luhrmann had gained fame as a movie director, making worldwide hits out of the music-driven romance *William Shakespeare's Romeo + Juliet* and the musical *Moulin Rouge!*

For *La Bohème*, Luhrmann's first Broadway show, Joe endured seven callbacks over six months. "Finally, the last callback was at a roller rink and we had to skate, which was real confusing. I didn't know what I was doing with the roller skates, but my dad knew what to do and he found me the best roller-skating coach in New Jersey. For two days in a row, six hours a day, we worked so hard. First, it was me trying to stand up, and by the end I was doing spins in the air!"

"I learned how to work a stage," Joe told *People* of his experience with the splashy show. "The director was really hard on me, but it was something I really loved and he will always be in my book as someone who helped me to perform," Joe said in *Life Story* in Winter 2008.

What happened next, Joe told *Life Story*, was that he "became a Broadway kid [who] wanted to dance all the time and sing. I'd walk into a grocery store and sing, 'Those are tacos!' It got worse and worse in every store I walked into. An interesting time for me."

For his part, oldest brother Kevin was allowed to go to New York City alone by age sixteen. Instead of using the privilege to goof off, shop, or meet new friends to hang around with, he used it to get to and from important auditions.

Then, in 2004, the guys were signed to Columbia Records after Nick—then billed as Nicholas—was briefly signed as a solo Christian-music artist. It was the culmination of their shared dream.

"I've always loved music," Nick told *Bop*'s June/July 2007 issue. "One night I was just like, 'Hey, guys, do you want to write a song?' We wrote our first song together and it got us signed to a record label." That song, "Please Be Mine," was so good that it was later included on their major-label debut.

Nick told *Twist* in March 2007, "My [label] was like, 'This is brilliant! Let's make it a brother act!'" Kevin said, "We never expected this to happen. Me and Joseph were always hoping that maybe we could get a song on Nicholas's record. We never thought about it as a brother group, but when it happened, it felt so right."

"When we're writing together, we're really open to each other's ideas," Nick told *Billboard* in June 2008, "which I think is really important when you're writing songs. No one can be closed-minded, because then nothing is going to work. For us, it's really just one of our passions. It's kind of our roots."

Their songwriting—a skill honed at the urging of their parents—was a primary reason why the boys were even given a chance at Columbia Records. They met with execs and wrote songs for them on the spot. Denise told *People* she believes her sons were signed not because they are great performers (which they are), but because they showed songwriting talent while being observed around a piano together.

But we all know that another reason the guys were signed was that their parents had nurtured their creativity all along and encouraged their aspirations. In the same way that the Jonas Brothers are a family band, it took their whole family to get them to where they are today.

And where the Jonas Brothers are today is on top of the world!

a matter of faith!

The Jonas Brothers rock, but are not your typical rock band—for starters, they're Christians who stand up for clean living and personal responsibility. Their faith is a big reason why a grassroots fan base sprang up.

"My parents are very strict, but also very trusting," Kevin said to *Bop* in March 2007. "We hope to be good role models," he continued in the magazine's February 2008 issue. "Parents won't have to worry about us doing crazy things onstage like cursing. It's just great that we can have a rock show that everyone can enjoy."

And in addition to their parents' watchful eyes, "We know the bloggers are watching, so we have to be careful and not do anything stupid," he also told *CosmoGIRL!* in Summer 2008.

Still, the brothers do try to walk a fine line between being honest about their values without coming off as too preachy. "On a personal level, faith is extremely important," Kevin Sr. told *Rolling Stone*. "But I kind of cringe every time I read references to them being a Christian band, for the simple reason that they don't sing Christian music. Probably because of my background, the boys get lumped into the Christian-music genre. But it isn't their genre."

One of the most visible manifestations of their beliefs is their steadfast insistence on wearing "purity rings," jewelry designed to remind young people to avoid intimate behavior prior to marriage. The boys have all worn the ring for years, and each did it on his "own personal time," Kevin reported.

"A lot of people ask us [if we're married] because we all wear a ring on our left hand," Kevin said in an interview with m in July 2007. "But it's not true!" Joe said, "It's basically a part of us. It's cool! Our fans have even started to cling to the idea, and we're happy to help out."

As the only famous males associated with this trend, the JoBros have had to answer questions on the topic over and over.

"Why is the world so freaked out that we have standards?" Nick wondered in People. Still, the guys don't want their rings to intimidate their fans or to set impossible-to-live-up-to standards.

fans in Popstar! in April 2008, "It fell off on vacation . . . at the wave pool at the Atlantis, in the Bahamas. I'm waiting for the new one to come in the mail. It's a little bit of a bummer. Mine is still there, just not physically . . . I want the exact same one again. It'll be back very soon!"

Nick had previously lost his first ring on a water-tubing trip, getting a new one made at Walt Disney World. His ring has "poned" inscribed on it (check "JoBros A to Z" at the back of this book if you don't know the definition) . . . perhaps he means that his willpower is poning any temptation to go back on his vow!

At the 2008 MTV Video Music Awards, presenter Russell Brand made fun of the Jonases for their rings,

Everything gets overanalyzed for us. We watch what we do, and we do our best to be good guys.

"First of all, we're not perfect," Nick admitted in Popstar! in October 2008. "We're not perfect guys." Joe said, "Everywhere you go, you're thinking to yourself, 'Put that cup down because it might be perceived as something bad when it's Diet Coke.' Everything gets overanalyzed for us. We watch what we do, and we do our best to be good guys."

But the rings have had a potent effect on fans, who have made the manufacture of custom purity or promise rings into a booming new industry.

When fans noticed Kevin had stopped wearing his purity ring in late 2007, rumors swirled. But he reassured

leading fellow presenter Jordin Sparks to stick up for them. The controversy was embarrassing for the boys, who have since said they still do think Brand is very funny.

The final word on those rings?

"We've talked about it enough," Nick told a Rolling Stone reporter. "We'd rather focus on the music and move on . . . the rings are a reminder to live a life of values. It's about being a gentleman, treating people with respect and being the best guys we can be."

But it's unlikely that we've heard the last of the boys' faith—it's a central part of their lives that fuels many of their actions.

ALL ABOUT NICK:
his short-lived solo career revealed!

"It all started with Nicholas," Kevin told *Tiger Beat* in July 2006. "He was working on a solo project, and Joseph and I were like, 'Maybe I can write a song with Nick and get it on the album!'"

It's true! Nick—then known personally and professionally as Nicholas—started creating his own contemporary Christian tunes, including one called "Joy to the World (A Christmas Prayer)" that he finished in 2002. The song impressed executives at INO Records the following year, and he was signed to a deal. His first single as a solo act was "Dear God," followed by "Joy to the World." This led to a very limited release of a self-titled album containing those songs plus "Time for Me to Fly" (later adapted on a Jonas Brothers record), "Appreciate," "When You Look Me in the Eyes" (also updated into a JB song), "Higher Love," "Please Be Mine," "I Will Be the Light," "Don't Walk Away," "Crazy Kinda Crush on You," and "Wrong Again."

When "Joy to the World" was played nationally on Christian stations, Daylight/Columbia Records took notice and partnered with INO to try to make Nicholas into a Christian singing star.

But Columbia's president, Steve Greenberg, had different ideas once he found out there were two more brothers just like Nicholas at home. He encouraged the guys to become a true Top 40 rock band, and they decided as a family it would be a great opportunity.

As you can imagine, being signed as a solo act only to have your big brothers muscled into the equation would be hard for any kid.

"For a minute it was a little tough, and then it was all good when I realized how cool it would be to tour and record with my brothers," Nick said of his brothers' signing in *Life Story*.

"It would have been a lot different," Nick told *CosmoGIRL!* in Summer 2008 about the possibility of his solo career taking off instead of his career with the Jonas Brothers. "I'm really happy that I have them here with me."

What about a solo career revisited? Is it just a matter of time before Nick records his own music, minus his brothers? It's not like he's never thought of it.

"If I were to release a solo record, it would probably sound a little more funky than a Jonas Brothers album, a little more R&B and soul-like. I love that kind of music and I would say that that's my style," Nick told *Life Story* in Winter 2008.

Could Nick be hinting at a future project?

DAY IN THE LIFE:
a peek at how the JoBros spend their not-so-average days and nights

MORNING!

Morning in the JoBros camp consists of wake-up calls, checking cell messages, showering and grooming, picking out clothes that everyone on the planet might see depending on who's taking their picture that day, and possibly doing a morning TV show like *Live with Regis and Kelly*.

Nick admitted that their mom is usually a human alarm clock for them when they're on tour. "She'll call us first thing in the morning and say, 'Hey, guys, what are you doing?'" He told *Teen* in Winter 2008. "I tell her I'm still in bed, but she'll keep asking questions."

Bad hair days happen to superstars, too! Nick told *Teen* in Summer 2008 that when he wakes up in the morning, he looks "like I have a huge afro." Joe jokes that he wakes up looking "like Orlando Bloom," while Kevin can only judge himself to be "gross" that early.

And, well, the boys don't always have the healthiest breakfasts when they're on the road. If they're in the South, they love to eat at Waffle House,

but "I usually start my day with the most chocolatey cereal," Joe told *Teen* in Winter 2008 (prior to endorsing the more health-conscious Breakfast Breaks). "But doughnuts are the ultimate treat." Nick told *Teen* in Summer 2008, "I have an energy drink when I wake up and a coffee when I eat breakfast." Wonder what Kevin does as soon as he wakes up? "Call room service for a big pot of coffee," he told *Teen* in Winter 2008. One of his fave java indulgences is vanilla chai.

But Kevin's not the one who could use a caffeine boost in the morning the most! His brother Joe is *definitely* not a morning person.

"When I wake up, I like to chill out and take my time," Joe said, defending himself in *Tiger Beat* in April 2007. "Everybody else is in a rush to take a shower and get ready, but I'm not!"

"Say we have to get up at eight and have to be out the door at nine," Kevin told *Bop* in its June/July 2008 issue. "Joe's out by 9:05 and he's the first one up at 8 a.m.! He takes forever!"

> "When I wake up, I like to chill out and take my time," Joe said.

AFTERNOON!

"On all the tours [we've done], we've gone from school in the morning to radio, we'd go have lunch with someone that's important, then go do a show, do a signing, go to bed. It never stops," Nick told *Popstar!* in August 2006. "People don't just get a million dollars off of a photo shoot. It just doesn't happen that way!"

They try to have lunch around 1 p.m., with Kevin's fave dish being a grilled chicken sandwich or chicken Caesar salad or even pizza from Pitfire Pizza in Burbank or Eclectic in North Hollywood if they're home in Cali.

Homeschooling would also occasionally get sandwiched into their afternoons, too, because it's something the guys took seriously. Kevin and Joe have graduated by now, but not without a few years of hard work. "We really have to apply ourselves to focus every day to get a certain amount of work done," Nick told *Bop* in December 2007. "If we have a break where we're not recording or anything, we'll take advantage of that time and get work done."

The guys choose all their own clothes after being presented with possible outfits by their stylist, Michelle Tomaszewski!

NIGHT!

The Jonas Brothers tour more than any of their young pop/rock peers, meaning their evenings are often . . . showtime! They're usually arriving at the venue by 6 p.m., assuming a 7 p.m. show. Backstage, they eat light (Nick will just grab an energy drink) and goof around with each other, but there's precious little time for that. Instead, they're often pulled into band meetings about that night's show or about new offers.

Then—after they blow their fans' minds with one of their legendary concerts—it's often time for a meet-and-greet around 9 p.m. if they haven't already done one prior to rockin' out.

What's next? "Most of the time we roll right after the concert, and then we get food," Joe told *People*. The guys are likely to return to their hotel and order burgers and ice cream from room service—never all at once, mind you, they like to order "like four times," Nick told *People*. They will play games like Halo if all three are hanging together.

Late at night, Nick likes to grab his guitar and unwind while being creative in the back of the tour bus or in his hotel room. He sometimes, but rarely, watches TV (he's partial to *Family Guy*).

Just before he turns in, the last thing he does is "read my Bible and pray," as reported to *Teen* in Summer 2008. Joe also says he prays—and eats—while Kevin admits to remaking his bed!

Wait . . . does this mean that the Jonas Brothers don't stay out late partying? Correct! When they're touring, there is *no* time for partying. "We're usually on the bus with our parents," Joe told *Bop* in December 2007. "We can't even go to the movies with our friends if we're still on the bus . . . We have to go to bed early because we have to wake up early."

Kevin is the closest thing to a night owl in the group. "My nighttime *starts* at 11 p.m.," he told *Life Story*. "I don't have trouble sleeping; I can fall asleep immediately, but I choose to stay up . . . I know it sounds weird, but I figure if I can go to bed at 11 or stay up for three more hours and enjoy my time, you know I'm going to stay up!"

which jonas would be your ideal BFF?

Keep track of how many of each color you answer YES to!

○ If someone tells me a secret, I never spill the beans— my mouth is a vault!

○ Going out for dessert and playing video games is the ideal afternoon!

○ My friends think of me as not only their pal, but also their protector!

○ I think that guys and girls can be "just friends" without romance!

○ It breaks my heart if I accidentally do something to make people mad!

○ If someone makes fun of me, I tend to take it to heart!

○ The best times of my life have been times I've spent with my family!

○ I can definitely take a joke, but I prefer to dish them out!

○ "Bossy" is just another word for having your act together!

○ When people talk about my business, I get really steamed!

○ I love pranking people and they're always totally shocked!

○ I love shopping with friends, but I have no problem doing it alone!

**Mostly Blue:
NICK!**

You and Nick are peas in a pod! You can look forward to intimate meetings, secret in-jokes and creativity retreats that produce new songs, poetry, and comedy videos!

**Mostly Red:
JOE!**

You're most likely to bond with Joe! Your goofball sense of humor and sensitivity make you the ideal friend for the outgoing singer. Just be careful...Joe thinks guys and girls always end up dating!

**Mostly Purple:
KEVIN!**

Your most ideal friendship match is the mature Kevin! You and he place a premium on loyalty and enjoy the art of good conversation just as much as catching a cool movie!

If you tied, that means you'd make a great friend to more than one or all of the JoBros!

21

take the ultimate jonas trivia test!

1. What unusual snack did the kitchen crew on *Camp Rock* make for the Jonas Brothers?

A. Cream cheese on white bread rolled with bacon in maple syrup

B. Salmon patties with pimento

C. Corn chips with green chile salsa

D. Graham crackers with vanilla frosting and Red Hots

2. What did Joe get for his 19th birthday?

A. His dream car

B. A motorcycle

C. An antique watch

D. The new iPhone

3. Kevin told *Tiger Beat* this gives him "a chill up his spine" and "the worst headache." What was it?

A. Hearing a singer who's off pitch

B. Seeing flashing lights

C. Sitting too close to the speakers

D. Sleeping in a moving vehicle

4. Which Jonas claimed to *J-14* in December 2007 that he can balance a tricycle on his foot?

A. Kevin

B. Nick

C. Joe

D. Frankie

5. Which Jonas told *People* he can't live without "my Bible, my guitar and a notepad to write down my thoughts"?

A. Denise

B. Nick

C. Kevin

D. Joe

6. How many guitars does Nick own?

A. 8

B. 6

C. 1

D. 25

7. What band did the Jonas Brothers play in *Camp Rock*?

A. Connected

B. Busted

C. Connect 3

D. 3 of Hearts

8. What did Joe steal from the White House?

A. Hand towels with the presidential crest

B. Two antique silver candy dishes

C. A U.S. flag-embroidered pillow

D. Hand soap with George Bush's face on it

9. What is Nick's most prized possession?

A. The gold watch he got for his 16th birthday

B. A Team USA jersey signed by Roger Clemens

C. An antique guitar his grandfather used to play

D. The first Prada shoes he ever got

10. The first #1 song on iTunes for the Jonas Brothers was . . .

A. "Burnin' Up"

B. "Year 3000"

C. "S.O.S."

D. "When You Look Me in the Eyes"

11. In order to fall asleep, Joe demands that his room be . . .

A. Completely dark

B. As hot as a sauna

C. Freezing cold

D. Scented with candles

12. What do the JoBros mean when they refer to their "condos"?

A. Their beds on their tour bus

B. Their rooms in their new Dallas house

C. Their various recording studios

D. Their friends' houses

13. What have the guys called their favorite dessert while on tour?

A. Chocolate pudding

B. Rice pudding

C. Vanilla ice cream

D. Cheesecake

14. What fake name has Kevin used when checking into hotels?

A. Teddy Geiger

B. Mr. Ketchup

C. Mr. Geraldo

D. Josephine Tibbs

15. What is Nick's favorite breakfast cereal?

A. Wheaties

B. Frosted Flakes

C. Cheerios

D. Rice Krispies

16. Which video was #1 on *TRL* during the JoBros' first visit on March 1, 2006?

A. "Sorry" by Madonna

B. "The Real Thing" by Bo Bice

C. "L.O.V.E." by Ashlee Simpson

D. "Mandy" by the Jonas Brothers

17. In "Year 3000," who is "doing fine"?

A. My best friend Lesley

B. Your great-great-great-granddaughter

C. President Barack Obama

D. Mickey Mouse

18. In the video for "Hold On," what does one of Joe's buttons say?

A. "Let's Have Good Clean Fun"

B. "Let's Be Careful Out There"

C. "Let's Go Crazy"

D. "Let's Not and Say We Did"

19. In the original *J.O.N.A.S* pilot, who was the villain?

A. Miley Cyrus

B. Global warming

C. The biggest roach ever

D. Dr. Harvey Fleischman, an evil dentist

20. For what superfamous singer did the JoBros' bodyguard Big Rob once work?

A. Selena Gomez

B. Zac Efron

C. Britney Spears

D. T.I.

21. When did the Jonas Brothers launch their MySpace page?

A. July 2004

B. July 2005

C. July 2006

D. April 2006

22. What did Joe used to want to be when he grew up?

A. Doctor

B. Stand-up comic

C. Lawyer

D. Minister

23. Which band inspired Nick to play the guitar?

A. All-American Rejects

B. Fall Out Boy

C. Switchfoot

D. Bon Jovi

24. What do fans of *Camp Rock* mail to Kevin Jonas as an in-joke based on a line from the movie?

A. Wiffle balls

B. Trophies

C. Apples

D. Birdhouses

25. Which team was Nick on during the 2008 Disney Channel Games?

A. Blue

B. Red

C. Yellow

D. Green

ANSWERS

1. A	6. A	11. A	16. A	21. A
2. B	7. C	12. A	17. B	22. B
3. A	8. A	13. D	18. A	23. B
4. C	9. B	14. C	19. D	24. D
5. B	10. C	15. C	20. C	25. B

Brother Bashing: Do They Fight?

As close as Kevin, Joe, and Nick are, they do have their disagreements!

"It's always something random like, 'Don't touch my guitar, who stole my Sidekick charger, who's gonna play with our little brother next . . .?'" they said to *Twist* in July 2006. "We talk over one another!" Kevin said. "Our parents have to make us take turns."

"We used to fight about who got the

front seat. That argument will never stop," Joe told *Twist*'s October/November 2006 issue.

Other points of contention are similarly trivial.

"The other night, Kevin was staying in my room because we had friends over and I had this thing that plugs in all my stuff to my room," Nick told *Popstar!* in January 2008. "It's like this big thing that I worked on for hours, and he unplugged it and plugged his stuff in! I was like, 'What are you doing? This is not cool!' Kevin was like, 'No, I'm not going to take them out!'"

See, Kevin—as the oldest bro—hates being told what to do by Nick or Joe.

Surprisingly, one of the easiest ways for Nick and Joe to annoy Kevin is to ask him advice about girls! In *Tiger Beat* in December 2006, Joe said, "Kevin's like the romantic king, so we'll go to him with everything girl-related, like our clothes and stuff: 'Does this look good to you?' Or even text messages—'Hey, Kevin, how does this sound?' And he'll be like, 'Joe, leave me alone!'"

"We really don't fight," Kevin tried to convince *J-14* in March 2008. Their arguments do sound pretty silly. "We have tons of socks, so that's the only thing we really fight about. It's like, 'Why are you wearing my socks?' Because I have the most comfortable socks, and I know when the socks they're wearing are mine," Joe said of his favorite Lacoste footwear. Nick admitted he guards his socks at home in a drawer, saying, "If anybody wears my socks, I flip out."

When they were younger, they would sometimes pick fights out of boredom— and just because they could!

"I think we all have a general idea of how to annoy each other," Nick said to *Tiger Beat* in December 2006. "We'll just think of what would annoy us and then

we're like, 'Okay, I bet this will work for them, too!'"

One source of tension involves competitions of any kind, which tend to bring out the wild man in Nick. "Nick J is the competitive one," Kevin told *Popstar!* in April 2008. "Like in Wiffle ball, he cannot lose!" Nick agreed, saying, "Losing is impossible for me!" Still, he refuses to go along with the idea that he throws huge tantrums. "The deal is it's only happened like three times and to them, they have, like, a perception now that it happens every time. So, like, even when I don't *freak* out about a game or something, they're like, 'Whoa! Calm down!' And I'm like, 'I'm fine!'"

Despite these rare blowups, the guys seem to be genuine in their affection and admiration for one another. Asked by *Tiger Beat* in its January/February 2008 issue to say what they admired about their bros, Kevin picked Joe's gift for comedy, Joe cited Nick's ability to be "very kind and nice" and Nick said, "I admire that Kevin wears those shoes all the time and does flips onstage in them."

As Nick said to *Tiger Beat* in June 2008, "We're working together all the time, so what's the point of being angry?"

their amazing albums!

Once the Jonas Brothers were signed to Columbia Records by Steve Greenberg, he immediately coached the guys, telling them to check out groups like Generation X, the Ramones, and Sham 69—hardcore punk rockers from the past. They did, and those influences are easy to hear on their debut disc, *It's About Time*.

But it wasn't as easy as just listening to some music and then cooking up their own—it took the boys about eighteen months to record *It's About Time*, including lots of back-and-forth on its creative direction.

Ultimately, the album was considered too weak by nervous executives, resulting in the addition of two songs at the insistence of the label—"What I Go to School For" and "Year 3000." Both of these songs had been written, performed, and released in the UK by the locally popular boy band Busted (who were unknown in the U.S., so their songs were considered fair game for reinvention), and were seen as more potentially hit-worthy. Both songs underwent lyrical revisions to avoid anything offensive (the original "What I Go to School For" was about crushing on a twenty-three-year-old teacher; Joe dedicated it

27

to the third-grade teacher he'd had a crush on back then) and the guys did get to choose punkier arrangements to make them their own.

Not that the Jonas Brothers are against doing cover versions of other artists' songs. But as Nick told *Popstar!* in May 2008, "The danger with covering great music is that if you don't do it as good as the artist did it originally, it's not good for you. So we made a promise to ourselves that we would never cover a Beatles song or, like, a Jackson 5 song or a Stevie Wonder song." One song he'd still like to reinvent? "There's a song by the Osmonds called 'One Bad Apple.' Awesome song!"

Even with the Busted songs added, the band chose to release the rockabilly number "Mandy" as their first single. "Mandy" was the last song the guys wrote for *It's About Time*. "We loved it; we found the sound we wanted and we ran with it," Kevin told *Life Story*.

The "Mandy" of the title is Mandy Van Duyne, their childhood friend (and Joe's former girlfriend). Mandy told *Fans' Choice: Jonas Brothers—Living the Dream*, "We were in the Jonas kitchen with their whole family and my family. After they played it, I think I was in shock, so I asked them to play it again . . . and again!"

It was one of the guys' favorite songs, too. "'Mandy' is a very fun song! It's very high energy and makes you want to get up and dance," Nick told *Popstar!* in January 2006.

Ondi Timoner, who had directed an acclaimed rock documentary called *DiG!* about seven years in the lives of two bands (the Brian Jonestown Massacre and the Dandy Warhols), was hired by Columbia to shoot not one but *three* videos for "Mandy," in order to attract as much attention as possible for the fledgling act.

The boys enjoyed their three-part video shoot . . . but it was hard on their dad—literally! "On the set of our 'Mandy' video, Kevin was doing one of his guitar spins and hit our dad in the head with his guitar!" the guys told *m* in July 2006.

The song proved popular enough to get the boys on MTV's *TRL*. "We flipped out! My dad got the e-mail and we all jumped up and down!" Nick told *Popstar!*

Along with the single "Mandy," the rest of the album

was a source of pride for the Jonas Brothers. "If people have a bad day at school, they can come back to their room, put our disc in, listen to it, go out and face the world again!" Nick told *Popstar!* in July 2006.

Nick used to love playing "What I Go to School For," until they got older and retired most of the tracks from this album.

"Time for Me to Fly" was one of the first songs the guys wrote together. Joe told *Life Story* it was about "forgetting your worries," and Kevin deemed it to be one of their most inspirational songs.

"Year 3000," one of the last songs added, became a late-breaking hit for the boys—and it's still on their playlist in concert.

"One Day at a Time" was about "missing someone, and every day you're just waiting for the next time you'll see that person," Nick told *Life Story*. Kevin said he loved this "amazing slow song."

The reggae-sounding "6 Minutes" proved hot during their concerts. It was not written by the boys, but Kevin loved the hook even though the original songwriter denied their request to add anything to the lyrics.

"You Just Don't Know It" was written in collaboration with Desmond Child. Joe called it a "stalker love song."

"I Am What I Am" was usually their opening song in concert. The guys hated it when they first heard it, but fell for it over time.

"Underdog" was, to Nick, "an awesome song" that was changed from being very acoustic guitar–oriented to more of a rocked-up headbanger.

The song "7:05" was one of Nick's favorite early tunes after he came up with a piano part and the guys wrote around that. "I love that song," Joe told *Life Story*, "because it has such a great story in it, and you can pinpoint every single situation that makes it up."

"Please Be Mine" was the song that got them signed, so they will always love it. "We were really fighting for that to be on the album, because we were working on someone else's songs on a lot of the tracks," Joe remembered in *Life Story*. "The song was so important to us."

> **"As crazy as it sounds, not *being* successful was the best thing that could have happened."**

But even though they finally had a killer album ready to go, times were tough—Columbia kept bumping the album's release date month after month.

Unfortunately, Greenberg—who'd been their champion—had left the company, which meant that the Jonas Brothers were musical orphans. It seemed the album wouldn't come out at all, but it finally saw the light of day in August 2006. Reports conflict as to exactly how many exist, but only about 62,000 were officially sold. Original copies of *It's About Time* are now going for over $150 on eBay.

With their album bombing, the Jonas Brothers were dropped by Columbia, leaving their future as a band uncertain. The boys were devastated and their growing fan base was shocked—was this the end of the Jonas Brothers?

Even though Columbia dropped the band, there were no hard feelings. The guys' manager, Phil McIntyre, told the *Wall Street Journal* that Columbia had done "an incredible job of identifying the talent. And they believed in the project and gave us room to develop as performers." But Columbia was not set up to get a youthful group like the Jonas Brothers out to the masses.

The guys began to look for a silver lining in their predicament. Nick said that being between labels was a blessing in disguise. "We as a band found it really cool that we had the time to grow musically. We did have a lot of time." And as we all know, *It's About Time*.

"There's never a day we're not doing something," Kevin told *Twist* in April 2008. They kept busy writing and perfecting their craft after deciding not to give up.

Then something amazing happened—Radio Disney put "Year 3000" in heavy rotation. "As soon as that happened, the song entered the Top 10 on iTunes and our MySpace comments doubled," Kevin noted in a press release. "It was almost impossible to keep up with the new friend requests!"

30

Impressed by a raucous audition that saw Joe rocking out on top of a Disney exec's desk, Hollywood Records—the Walt Disney company that had just had great success with Hilary Duff and Jesse McCartney—signed the Jonas Brothers, giving them a second chance.

Unlike Columbia, Hollywood was well equipped to saturate young consumers with the sounds and even images of the Jonas Brothers—for starters, the boys appeared on Radio Disney 24/7 and scored a spot on the soundtrack for *Meet the Robinsons* with a catchy version of the '80s hit "Kids in America" remade as "Kids of the Future."

By the summer of 2007, Jonas Brothers songs accounted for 9 percent of all requests made to Radio Disney. "Boys identify with them, and girls love them because they're cute," the senior vice president and general manager of Radio Disney said at the time.

The more the kids saw and heard of them, the more they liked the Jonas Brothers.

"As crazy as it sounds, *not* being successful was the best thing that could have happened," Nick told *CosmoGIRL!* in Summer 2008. "We grew as a band and as a team, and got a lot stronger."

In the end, it's not only about time—it's also about believing in yourself.

test your knowledge of...
it's about time!

1. What British group originally sang both "What I Go to School For" and "Year 3000"?

A. U2

B. Busted

C. McFly

D. Oasis

2. Before its lyrics were changed for the JoBros, "What I Go to School For" was about a boy crushing on who?

A. His female BFF

B. His sister's BFF

C. His ex-GF

D. His teacher

3. What was the JoBros' first-ever single?

A. "Mandy"

B. "Please Be Mine"

C. "Year 3000"

D. "I Am What I Am"

4. What was the first song the Jonas Brothers ever wrote together?

A. "Please Be Mine"

B. "Dear Diary"

C. "Mandy"

D. "One Day at a Time"

5. Which song from the album has a reggae beat?

A. "Mandy"

B. "6 Minutes"

C. "You Just Don't Know It"

D. "Time for Me to Fly"

6. Who sings lead on "Time for Me to Fly"?

A. Nick

B. Joe

C. Kevin

D. Frankie

7. In which order, from left to right, are the brothers shown standing on the CD cover?

A. Nick, Joe, Kevin

B. Nick, Kevin, Joe

C. Kevin, Joe, Nick

D. Joe, Nick, Kevin

8. Which song do the guys think of as a "stalker love song"?

A. "You Just Don't Know It"

B. "Underdog"

C. "6 Minutes"

D. "Mandy"

9. Where does the girl from the song "Underdog" live?

A. Next door

B. Up the block

C. In her own little world

D. In fear

10. The JoBros are on the cover of which two fake magazines in the video for "Year 3000"?

A. *Music Mania* and *Future Today*

B. *Platinum Times* and *Rockit*

C. *Best Beats* and *Rocked Up*

D. *Tune* and *Rockboard*

ANSWERS

		4. A
	7. C	3. A
10. D	6. A	2. D
9. A	5. B	1. B

"Once we signed over to Hollywood Records, we found a family that really took care of us and believed in us and supports us in the way of releasing our songs and pushing them," Kevin Jonas reflected in *Popstar!* in May 2008.

Joe has said that once they were brought aboard by Disney, everything changed. "Before the Disney push, we were seeing a slight change," he told *Life Story*. "But right away, after they put the first video on Disney Channel, on our MySpace page we suddenly had hundreds of thousands of friend requests in an hour. It was just unbelievable to see how crazy the response was. Our fan base grew faster than ever. We had so many more fans in the course of one month than we did in two years."

Along with helping to get the Jonas Brothers introduced to a waiting audience via hyping up "Year 3000," Hollywood Records also nurtured the Jonas Brothers' songwriting aspirations.

"When we signed to Hollywood, we told the label, 'Hey, we have some demos of songs we've been writing for the past year and a half.' We thought it'd be so funny to just record those songs for the album to see what we could get away with. But those turned out to be the songs on the record!" Kevin recalled.

Amazingly, the guys were allowed to write all of the songs, with cowriting credits going to more seasoned pros like Bleu ("That's Just the Way We Roll") and P. J. Bianco ("When You Look Me in the Eyes"). "As brothers, we just know how to work together," Nick explained.

Hollywood hooked the guys up with top producers and streamlined the recording process in a way that shocked the Jonas clan. The record took exactly three weeks to make as opposed to *It's About Time*'s eighteen-month timeline. Nick told *Bop* in September 2007 that four or five of the songs on the

JONAS BROTHERS
(HOLLYWOOD RECORDS)
AUGUST 7, 2007

"S.O.S."
"Hold On"
"Goodnight and Goodbye"
"That's Just the Way We Roll"
"Hello Beautiful"
"Still in Love with You"
"Australia"
"Games"
"When You Look Me in the Eyes"
"Inseparable"
"Just Friends"
"Hollywood"
"Year 3000"
"Kids of the Future"

album took only fifteen minutes to record!

In February 2007, the guys found themselves in Seedy Underbelly, a recording studio, with producer John Fields. They were awed by Fields, who had worked on Switchfoot's record *The Beautiful Letdown* as well as with artists like Rooney and Pink. "John lives rock music," Joe said at the time. "We always thought it would be so cool to work with him."

While recording, the guys had a lot of fun—too *much* fun?—in the studio. Nick told *Tiger Beat Celebrity Spectacular!* in Summer 2008, "Joe always tries to make us laugh, so sometimes you'll hear a random laugh in the background of a song. There's one time where Joe messed up the lyrics, I was rolling on the ground laughing so hard."

"It was one of the best experiences," Kevin raved to *Life Story*. "We were there recording and were involved from the first beat of the drum and first time something was put on tape, right through to the end."

The finished product had everyone at the label thrilled—not to mention the excitement it gave the Jonas Brothers, who by all accounts felt they had finally achieved their dream.

"We're always writing new music on tour or at home," Joe told *Popstar!* in March 2007, before the release of *Jonas Brothers*. "In the past two months, we've written, like, 10 songs. It's been awesome!" Nick said their sound was "the same for sure. I think just chord-wise and lyrically, it's more interesting, which is cool. It draws you in. It'll be good. I'm excited about it."

The only dark cloud? Some fans were annoyed (and some were relieved) when the aggressive, angry breakup song "Move On," which had been leaked online earlier, was left off *Jonas Brothers* at the last minute, replaced by the less shocking "Inseparable." Joe told *Popstar!* in November 2007, "The switch, to us, we're totally cool with it. There's no real reason why it was taken off. It will definitely be used later on. It's all good."

"Move On" wasn't the only song kicked to the curb. Plain White T's singer Tom Higgenson told *J-14* in December 2007 that he'd collaborated with the guys on a song for the record, but that their mutual label, Hollywood, had cut it at the last second. "I love those guys," he said. "I think my song was a lot better than some of the songs that did make it."

But the songs that *did* make the cut were embraced by fans.

"Hold On" was the lead single and was coincidentally one of the first songs written for the CD. Joe told *Life Story* this song was about always being able to "find the light if you look hard enough."

Kevin's favorite song on the record, "S.O.S."—written entirely by Nick—was a fan fave out of the box, and would become the album's second single. Nick told *Life Story* that he wrote this one "out of some personal experiences; things that I went through that were kind of tough, but everything worked out . . . I always write better songs when I have a strong inspiration for them, and for this song I had a really strong inspiration."

"The real story behind it is there is this girl who came to town to hang and just wasn't cool and messed everything up," Nick told *Bop* in November 2007. "When I really have inspiration for something, it's really easy for me to write a song. 'S.O.S.' was written in 15 minutes, as well as 'Still in Love With You' and 'Inseparable.'"

"S.O.S." took off on radio, but not without some help. Nick told *Popstar!* in January 2008, "When I first heard about 'S.O.S.' being on Z100, I freaked out, because we were in Toronto and we heard they were going to spin the record, and because we told people on MySpace, 'Make sure you listen,' they called in and voted so many times that it made it to #3 on the countdown, which was totally crazy. The following night, we got the call that it was #1—so we were totally psyched about that!"

"When You Look Me in the Eyes" was the album's final single, a power ballad that caught fire at Top 40 radio. The song's inspiration was said to come from the feeling of staring into a girl's eyes the first time a romantic spark happens. In this way, this song is a tribute to the millions of female fans the boys gained in 2007.

The song was originally written for Nick's solo album—it was one of the very first tunes the brothers cowrote. They loved it so much they never forgot it, adding it to their second album in a more polished, more grown-up form.

"Goodnight and Goodbye" is a breakup song that Kevin says "captures the moment when you're done with a crazy relationship." He also points out it's inspired by Nick's desire, when ending a relationship, to be able to just say, "Peace. I'm out of here."

"That's Just the Way We Roll" became like the new "Year 3000" for its crowd-pleasing, offbeat lyrics.

"It's about missing a girl while you're on tour and all you want is to get on a plane and fly to her," Joe said of "Hello Beautiful" in *Life Story*. The guys have said they love its acoustic sound.

"Still in Love With You" is another breakup song, but one that you could argue leaves the door open. Kevin, Joe, and Nick felt at the time this song's structure was a major step forward in their progress as artists.

As Joe told *Life Story*, "We love Australian accents—especially me—and if a girl has an accent (doesn't matter which kind), I'm probably in love with her." This might have something to do with the existence of the humorous song "Australia" on the album.

"Games" was inspired by the Police, the classic band the guys were listening to at the time, and the pop/reggae sound of that band bled into this song, which the guys actually wrote with some of their band members. Interestingly, the Jonas Brothers wrote "Games" while touring for the first time with Jesse McCartney, who at the time was the ultimate teen idol—little did they know, they were about to take his place!

"Inseparable," a last-minute addition to *Jonas Brothers*, is their long-distance relationship song. "One of the most rocking songs on the record," Joe observed in *Life Story*.

Fans obsessed with Niley—whether or not Nick Jonas was dating fellow teen star Miley Cyrus—were all over "Just Friends." Nick loves this song about a guy and a girl who are friends and the guy "is actually madly in love with the friend but can never admit it." It seems hard to deny this was inspired by his friendship with and/or courtship of Miley Cyrus!

Juicily enough, another big fan of "Just Friends" is . . . Nick's longtime rumored girlfriend Selena Gomez! "'Just Friends' by the Jonas Brothers is one of my favorite songs! It's sweet, but it's fun, and you can jump around to it!" she told *Twist* in August 2008.

The song "Hollywood" was planned as a bit of a tribute to their new label and newfound sense of freedom.

The remake of Kim Wilde's 1981 hit "Kids of America" as "Kids of the Future" was added to the album after being included in *Meet the Robinsons*. The guys actually felt this was a great transition song for them from their old sound to their slightly rockier new sound. It also helped that Hollywood decided to include "Year 3000" again on the album—since so few copies of *It's About Time* had been sold, it made sense that new fans would love to "discover" this song on their own.

"This album is so us," Joe said upon the release of *Jonas Brothers*. "The first one was us kind of coming into what the *Jonas Brothers* could be," Kevin clarified. "Whereas this one really shows off where we're at right now." For Nick's part, he summed everything up with his usual Yoda-like wisdom, saying, "We love what we're doing and we want to do it for a while."

Making things even more special, *Jonas Brothers* was the first album ever released in the CDVU+ ("CD view plus") format, a digital-music experience full of extras (seventy-five printable photos of the band, song lyrics, video segments, a letter from the guys) and downloads. It also came in environmentally friendly packaging.

"We're aiming for people our age," Joe said in a Hollywood Records press release just prior to the album's debut. "But we also wanna get kids younger than us," Nick added. Leaving no stone unturned, Kevin finished the thought with, "And older people, too."

They succeeded—*Jonas Brothers* was a Top 5 smash, going on to sell about 1.5 million copies. Its success helped them earn $12 million as a band in 2007, and it laid the groundwork for more great music to come.

test your knowledge of...
jonas brothers!

1. Which song is really about a girl who came to town to hang out with the guys but who messed everything up?

A. "S.O.S."

B. "Australia"

C. "When You Look Me in the Eyes"

D. "Hollywood"

2. What is "Hollywood" inspired by?

A. Their new home

B. Their new record label

C. Their obsession with celebrities

D. The realization of all their dreams

3. 3. Which movie used "Kids of the Future" on its soundtrack?

A. *The Chronicles of Narnia*

B. *Harry Potter and the Sorceror's Stone*

C. *Old School*

D. *Meet the Robinsons*

4. At four minutes and nine seconds, what is the longest song on *Jonas Brothers*?

A. "Hello Beautiful"

B. "When You Look Me in the Eyes"

C. "Kids of the Future"

D. "Games"

5. What was the song you could only get on the Wal-Mart edition of *Jonas Brothers*?

A. "Take a Breath"

B. "We Got the Party"

C. The Baby Bottle Pop theme song

D. "Out of This World"

6. What was the first single released from *Jonas Brothers*?

A "S.O.S."

B. "Hold On"

C. "When You Look Me in the Eyes"

D. "Inseparable"

7. In what order do the bros appear on the cover, from left to right?

A. Kevin, Nick, Joe

B. Kevin, Joe, Nick

C. Nick, Joe, Kevin

D. Nick, Kevin, Joe

8. Who produced the album?

A. The Jonas Brothers

B. Kevin Jonas Sr.

C. Johnny Wright

D. John Fields

9. What was the highest chart position for the album?

A. #1

B. #5

C. #10

D. #40

10. Name the caustic revenge song that was cut from the album at the last minute.

A. "Move Out"

B. "Move Up"

C. "Move On"

D. "Move It"

ANSWERS

1. A   3. D   5. C   7. A   9. B
2. B   4. B   6. B   8. D   10. C

"We just recorded new demos for the next album and they're cool! It's going to be the same core Jonas Brothers sound like 'S.O.S.', but with a little more dancing and just throwing the beats down," Joe told *Twist* in January 2008.

The album whose existence he was teasing would not see the light of day until August 2008. Named *A Little Bit Longer* after Nick's touching ballad of the same name, it represented yet another major leap forward for the guys.

"The songs are about more meaningful things than the last CD," Kevin observed to *m* in May 2008. "There are also fun and exciting songs like 'Burnin' Up,' which we sing during our concert now."

"It's a little more funky and still who we are as a pop-rock band," Nick told *J-14* in its May/June 2008 issue. "They're really fun songs."

Because of a lack of time, the Jonas Brothers recorded *A Little Bit Longer* on their Gibson Guitars–sponsored bus while knockin' 'em dead on the Look Me in the Eyes Tour.

"Pretty much we were writing all these songs when we were on tour," Joe said to *Billboard*, "and we didn't have time to go into a studio and record. There's a lot of time when you're on the tour bus where there's a lot of waiting around. We have like four hours in each day where we could really do something."

"I think we grew up on the road a little bit," Joe told *Billboard*. "It's not like we were immature and now we're changing our sound or anything like that, but we're getting older and I think we've learned more from life in the last couple of years."

"BB Good" became one of the band's favorites to do live on their Burning Up Tour because it's one of the album's only purely fun songs, with no angst.

"Burnin' Up" was everyone's pick as the lead single—and what a great decision that was! One of Kevin's favorite songs on the album, it went Top 5 on the *Billboard* Hot 100 chart,

A LITTLE BIT LONGER
(HOLLYWOOD RECORDS)
AUGUST 12, 2008

"BB Good"
"Burnin' Up"
"Shelf"
"One Man Show"
"Lovebug"
"Tonight"
"Can't Have You"
"Video Girl"
"Pushin' Me Away"
"Sorry"
"Got Me Going Crazy"
"A Little Bit Longer"

powered by an elaborate music video featuring a rap by their beloved bodyguard, Big Rob. Fans compared it to Maroon 5.

"Shelf," which sounds a lot like a Weezer track, was one of the tunes they'd previewed on their Look Me in the Eyes Tour, so they knew it was a winner.

Speaking of songs like "One Man Show," "Video Girl," "Tonight," and "Got Me Going Crazy," Nick said to *Popstar!* in May 2008, "There are some Elvis Costello influences as well as the Beatles. But there are a couple of songs that really do have that Prince vibe, and I think it's a little more funky but just more of us having a good time!"

The stripped-down "Lovebug" was one of the guys' preferred songs (and Nick's favorite, alongside "A Little Bit Longer") because it was one of the most unexpected on the record since it starts out as an old-fashioned–sounding love song (with Joe's tap dancing heard as percussion) and builds to a hard-rocking crescendo. They chose it as a single, and while it failed to became a major success, it garnered lots of attention and led to some high-profile live TV performances.

Kevin's favorite song on the album, according to *Bop* in October 2008, was "Can't Have You." He said, "I love that song. It's really special." Joe had a different pick. "For me, I would say a song called 'Sorry.' It's about being on tour and missing someone and you're just very sorry you can't be around."

"I wrote 'Can't Have You' about liking somebody, but when you can't have them you realize it's not worth it," Nick told *Twist* in July 2008. "'Sorry' is about being away from your crush . . . It's saying, 'I'm sorry I wasn't there to keep these promises, but you know that I still really care about you.'"

Interviewed by *m* for its October/November 2008 issue, Kevin said, "The songs on *A Little Bit Longer*, like 'Sorry,' are about getting through tough times. Because we were touring so much when we wrote this album, the songs are about being on the road and being away from the ones we love."

"Pushin' Me Away" is a heartfelt, uptempo number that was a huge hit on iTunes, helping to propel album sales later on. "'Pushin' Me Away,'" Kevin told *Twist* in July 2008, "shows a new side to who we are, and our fans are really catching on to it!"

Long before the rest of the album was complete, Nick had also begun working on a deeply personal song for the new record while on tour. It was personal because it addressed his battle with diabetes. When he first wrote it, it was entitled "You Don't Even Know."

Nick told *Twist* in March 2008, "I wrote it while we were filming *Camp Rock*. We've played it live a couple of times and it's overwhelming!" According to his interview with *People*, the song came about on one of the days when his blood sugar was haywire. "I was kind of bumming. I walked by this room in the hotel we were staying at, and it was so weird—all of the sudden there was this big ballroom with a piano in it. It was like a scene out of a movie. So I went in there, sat down at the piano and wrote the song. Later on I played it for the cast, and they all loved it."

When the guys made their final song choices for *A Little Bit Longer*—from dozens they'd recorded—Kevin said, "I think we were able to capture who we are with the songs we selected."

In the end, *A Little Bit Longer* scanned over a million copies and presented the Jonas Brothers as teen idols on the verge of rock 'n' roll cred crossover—exactly their goal as artists.

NICK'S SURPRISE ANNOUNCEMENT:
how diabetes changed (and didn't change) his life!

In the autumn of 2005, while touring with his brothers in Europe, Nick Jonas began to act totally out of character—he was suddenly cranky and lethargic. "I started experiencing weight loss, a bad attitude," he told *Twist* in July 2007.

"We went swimming and he took his shirt off, and I freaked," Joe said to *Rolling Stone*. "He looked like a skeleton."

Nick even fell asleep at a photo shoot one time, the week *Jonas Brothers* was released. "I looked at something, closed my eyes, and woke up an hour later. I heard someone say, 'Are you ready to do your first shot?' And I was like, 'Yeah.' But I had no idea where I was or anything. It was pretty hilarious."

"After the tour, we went to the doctor and found out I had diabetes," Nick said. "The first thing I asked the doctor was if I was going to die. It was crazy."

He told *Rolling Stone*, "I didn't know if we'd be able to continue as a band."

He spent three days in the hospital to assess his disease. Nick has type 1, which is when your body doesn't produce insulin, a hormone that's needed to turn sugar into energy. Without it, all the excess sugar can make those who suffer from the disease very sick or, if left untreated, they can die.

"It was hard. There were times I just didn't want to have it. It was a learning process." Nick had to introduce insulin into his body by wearing an OmniPod.

After his initial treatment, Nick said, it dawned on him that he would be just fine. He was equipped with an insulin pump connected to a wireless device in his pocket to monitor all his levels. Most of his junk food is sugar-free. Still, he pricks his finger daily about a dozen times to see if he needs to do anything to up his blood sugar. After he found out, it took him about nine months to feel normal again. "Once you

find a pattern with diabetes, you can have normalcy."

"Once my family felt we had it under control, we decided to tell the world!"

The big announcement happened at the Carnival for a Cure, an annual event held by the Diabetes Research Institute. Nick asked everyone in the room with diabetes to raise their hand . . . and shocked the crowd by raising his own hand! Fans were beside themselves with worry, but out of this public proclamation came a lot of good—kids became educated about diabetes, kids with diabetes found a powerful friend and advocate in Nick Jonas, and fans became motivated to raise money to fight the disease.

The disease also brought the Jonases even closer together. Kevin and Joe gave Nick all their support. "On the way to the hospital, Kevin and Joe looked up diabetes online. They knew more about it than I did before I got there! They're there for me all the time," Nick told *Twist* in July 2007.

"The feelings you go through are so vast," Nick's mom Denise told *Rolling Stone*. "There's grief, because he's lost his health. There's guilt—'What did I do to my child?' You're uneducated about what it is. Once I understood, I could release that."

Nick's diet is very important. He's allowed to have sugary things, but needs to be sure his body has enough insulin to convert that sugar in his blood into energy, balancing sugar intake with his intake of carbohydrates. Most importantly, he tries to maintain a consistent, nutritious diet.

There have been times when Nick's pump (and backup pump . . . and backup backup pump) hasn't worked, leading to stressful and time-consuming journeys to get him a working pump, but overall, Nick is living proof that diabetes is not the end of anything.

test your knowledge of ... a little bit longer!

1. The album is named for the song that Nick wrote about what issue?

A. Diabetes

B. Bullying

C. Global warming

D. Peer pressure

2. Which was the first single from *A Little Bit Longer* released to iTunes?

A. "Lovebug"

B. "Burnin' Up"

C. "Pushin' Me Away"

D. "Tonight"

3. How many copies did *A Little Bit Longer* sell in its first week of release?

A. 500,000+

B. 1,000,000+

C. 50,000+

D. 150,000+

4. What Beatles remake was only available on the Target version of *A Little Bit Longer*?

A. "Paperback Writer"

B. "Yesterday"

C. "Hello, Goodbye"

D. "Please Please Me"

5. Who raps on "Burnin' Up"?

A. Big Rob

B. Eminem

C. 50 Cent

D. T.I.

6. On which *A Little Bit Longer* song does popular bandmate Greg "Garbo" Garbowsky share a writing credit?

A. "Tonight"

B. "BB Good"

C. "Shelf"

D. "Burnin' Up"

7. Who wrote "Got Me Going Crazy"?

A. The Jonas Brothers

B. Nick Jonas

C. Kevin Jonas

D. Justin Timberlake

8. Which of these *A Little Bit Longer* songs was not played on the Burning Up Tour?

A. "Burnin' Up"

B. "BB Good"

C. "Sorry"

D. "Tonight"

9. Former Nick crush Camilla Belle stars in the video to which *A Little Bit Longer* song?

A. "Lovebug"

B. "Burnin' Up"

C. "Pushin' Me Away"

D. "Tonight"

10. The guys chose the final sequence of songs for *A Little Bit Longer* while filming what event?

A. *The Ellen DeGeneres Show*

B. *The Oprah Winfrey Show*

C. The Disney Channel Games

D. *Dick Clark's New Year's Rockin' Eve*

ANSWERS

10. C
9. A
8. C
7. B
6. A
5. A
4. C
3. A
2. B
1. A

EARLY YEARS ON THE ROAD!

The Jonas Brothers have not always been a stadium rock act—when they were first starting out, they could barely afford to tour at all! But their love of music and their desire to get themselves heard led them onto the road as often as possible.

Asked in *Popstar!* what makes the JoBros stand out, Kevin replied, "I think the fact that we're not a choreographed dance group and we write our [own] songs. We perform our songs and play all of the instruments. And I guess that allows us to perform in a way that really does show how we are as people. I think it's another way for people to connect with us."

From November 5 through December 17, 2005, the guys embarked on their first-ever formal tour, the Jonas Brothers Fall 2005 Promo Tour. They played small venues close to home, introducing themselves to fans and getting themselves used to life on the road.

At one gig, the guys even had to scrounge around and use the Click Five's equipment. "It was awesome getting to play their stuff! It's loud!" they told *Popstar!* in January 2006.

To keep costs low, they skipped lodging and sound checks. "We slept in vans, and our dad drove us overnight and for days in the van. He was the driver and we were our own crew," Kevin recounted to *Life Story* in Winter 2008. "We did this thing called the *School Tour* where we woke up at 3 a.m. every single morning and drove to the schools. We would load everything in and set up an entire P.A. system with one other guy. And we wouldn't stay in a hotel overnight."

They even skipped getting paid on some gigs—for the privilege of opening for Jesse McCartney, the Veronicas, or the Backstreet Boys, the exposure was the pay.

Part of that first tour (from December 6 through December 17) was a slot as the surprise opening act for the Cheetah Girls' Cheetah-licious Christmas Tour, putting them in the company of a powerful Disney-fueled act for the first time. They also met Aly & AJ on this tour, who would become friends of theirs for a time.

The tour was difficult, as was performing for a crowd

who had come for other acts. Some of their shows went well while others were marred by flaws.

"You can't bat a .500 every day," Kevin said to *Life Story* in Winter 2008. "Sometimes you come away thinking it was the best show ever, or sometimes you say, 'That was a good show, but it wasn't my favorite.' For us, we just enjoy going out there and giving it our all."

The exposure had some immediate, if limited, side effects.

"I was recognized at a mall in our town," Kevin told *Tiger Beat* in June 2007. "It was a little shocking someone could just know who you are without ever meeting them."

Small tours like theirs, as well as one-off dates, were not without their perks. "I'd have to say the Veronicas were a lot of fun!" Joe reported to *Popstar!* in August 2006 of their one-time touring buddies. "The last night, we kept waiting to prank the girls. They had this mascot stuffed kangaroo named Ninny. When they were loading up their gear, it was outside. I grabbed it and took it and just walked onto our tour bus and later told them we'd ransom it for $5 billion dollars!"

While touring with Aly & AJ, the guys spent a lot of time cracking jokes and pranking the girls. The biggest running joke came when the boys found out Aly & AJ call going to the bathroom "marshmallows." As a joke, someone on their crew filled the girls' bunks with actual marshmallows. They thought it had to be the Jonases, so they pelted the boys with them. Kevin said they also pretended to be the girls' guitar techs before a performance! "We went on stage and plugged in their guitars. We looked really serious, and they were so confused."

Next up, the guys got it together for the Jonas Brothers American Club Tour, which encompassed twenty-eight dates between January 28 and March 3, 2006. These gigs were very small (they sometimes played for only a dozen spectators). They were no overnight success story!

"Our savings were spent, credit cards were maxed out. We were selling T-shirts for gasoline money at every gig," Kevin Sr. told *People*.

Joe remembered their early days on the road as challenging, but character building, "We would play *Bamboozle* with, like, tons of other bands who have been making it for years, and we were the young kids on the block," he told *Popstar!* in May 2008. "And so it was just, 'Never give up!' And if you really love doing it, then just keep it up."

Then there were the inevitable squabbles caused by being so jam-packed together for so long. Nick spilled the beans to *Popstar!* in March 2007 on his distaste for Joe's messiness on the tour bus. "On the bus, his bunk is right above me but all his stuff will be in my bunk for some reason. And I'll be like, 'Why is your stuff in my bunk?' and he'll be like, 'Oh, I'm sorry!' But he'll just take it out of my bunk and put it in the floor!"

But these early touring experiences gave the boys confidence—and won over tons of new fans. Even the hardships were not enough to squelch their desire to get back out on the road.

When asked by *Tiger Beat* in July 2006 about his summer plans, Kevin said, "Touring! Maybe going to the beach, but all I really care about is touring." Nick added, "I can't wait for the warm weather and going on tour."

MARVELOUS PARTY TOUR

*N*ick told *Tiger Beat* in December 2007, "When we play a show, you never have to worry that I can only see one person in the audience. I see *everyone.*" Keeping that in mind, their next tour encouraged fans to dress up in a special way for the guys—and they definitely noticed!

Their third tour—and their first major effort—was called the Marvelous Party Tour. This was the outing that really captured fans' imaginations due to its memorable prom theme. Lasting from June 25 through October 21, 2007, the tour was made up of forty-six dates all over the country, a remarkable expansion from their earlier journeys.

Their first-ever headlining tour visited state fairs, medium-sized theaters, and clubs. The tour coincided

SET LIST

"Kids of the Future"
"That's Just the Way
  We Roll"
"Goodnight and
  Goodbye"
"Just Friends"
"Inseparable"
"Still In Love with
  You"
"Hello Beautiful"
"S.O.S."
"Games"
"Australia"
"Hollywood"
"Hold On"
"Year 3000"

with their deal to promote Baby Bottle Pops, the popular Topps candy, for which they recorded a commercial that got their faces out to potential fans in a big way. That candy deal was helpful in another, more concrete way—Disney persuaded Wal-Mart to display *Jonas Brothers* alongside Baby Bottle Pops in almost half (meaning over 2,000!) of its stores nationwide, guaranteeing huge exposure for the boys.

But it was the prom theme that was marketing genius, leading to sold-out dates.

"Our tour has a giant prom theme. Since we never had a prom, we are bringing the prom to everyone," Kevin told *J-14* in July 2007. Their ideal prom dates? Kevin chose Hayden Panettiere, Joe wanted Katharine McPhee, and Nick preferred Brenda Song.

Joe joked to *Tiger Beat* in November 2007 that his ideal prom outfit would include "a disco-ball helmet. I'm always like, 'It's time to have fun.'" Kevin's take on prom was, "The minute you walk into prom with me, I want you to have fun. I don't get nervous holding hands with a girl." Nick promised, "I'm gonna get dressed up, so it will be sweet if my date came dressed up, too. My favorite way to impress a girl is by singing to her. I want to serenade her, or at least try to."

Fans arrived at the shows in prom-style dresses—and their dates were the Jonas Brothers themselves.

"We'll see a girl who's cute and we have this talk-back mic that's on the stage. It only goes into each other's ears, so the audience can't hear it. We'll say, 'Dude, look! Do you see her? She's really cute!'" Nick told *Twist*.

The tour had its usual difficulties, but nothing insurmountable.

"There's always a certain point on tour where one person will get sick," Nick

how to catch their eye on tour!

Kevin listed for *J-14* in August 2008 the best ways to get the guys' attention if you're a fan in the audience at one of their concerts:

- Dress nicely!
- Have a great, funny sign!
- Scream louder than anyone!

said to *m* in December 2007. "And then everyone'll get sick! But we'd never cancel a show."

"I love that we get to travel all the time and not be sitting home doing nothing," Kevin told *Tiger Beat* in June 2008. And Joe loves being able to "go onstage and say ridiculous things. I can say funny things onstage and it's not a script."

Of course, eating on the road can be tough, but not if you're a growing boy who'll eat anything! "We like truck stops and we love Wendy's," Nick shared with *m* in December 2007. They had a lot of opportunities to sample the truck stops of the nation on the Marvelous Party Tour—it hit more states than any of their previous excursions. It also touched more hearts!

BEST OF BOTH WORLDS TOUR

The JoBros were demoted back to an opening act—but they had no complaints considering they were opening for Miley Cyrus, a close pal and the biggest touring act of the year! The Best of Both Worlds Tour lasted from October 18, 2007, through January 11, 2008, with the Jonas Brothers participating for fifty-four of the dates.

"It's true," Nick confirmed to *m* in December 2007 when rumors went around about the tour. "We're going to be singing the song 'We Got the Party' with Miley. It's the tune we sang on *Hannah Montana* with her. I'm not sure whether Miley will be singing as herself or Hannah. It's all very confusing!"

When the guys arrived to perform at the State Fair of Texas, it finally hit them just how *big* they'd gotten—traffic to the venue was so clogged with 20,000 vehicles that they were forced to take their first helicopter ride from the airport to the place they would play. According to *People Special Collector's Edition: All About the Jonas Brothers*, Nick said, "I thought, 'Wow, this is really awesome.' It was one of those moments where we just sat back in shock."

Working with Miley Cyrus—who Nick was secretly dating throughout the tour—was a joy for all of the brothers.

SET LIST

"Kids of the Future"
"Just Friends"
"That's Just the Way We Roll"
"Hello Beautiful"
"Goodnight and Goodbye"
"Hold On"
"S.O.S."
"We Got the Party" with Miley Cyrus as Hannah Montana

"Miley's one of my best friends," Joe told *m* in March 2008. "She works so hard all the time. She'll go on stage and play two sets, as Miley and as Hannah—altogether, it'll be like 30 songs! It's crazy." Nick agreed, saying, "Yeah, she's awesome. Miley's just a really cool girl. She's down to earth, and that's really important to me." Kevin likened her to the little sister they never had, a real "ball of energy!"

"Joe would battle Miley onstage," Kevin said to *People*. "They'd do mic tricks to see who was best in front of everyone. One time, they were doing it and all of a sudden Joe went down into a full split and came back up with his mic stand. Miley's mouth dropped like, 'I hate you.' It was hilarious!"

The brothers made sure their visuals for this tour were memorable—they wore red-accented suits and they engaged in even more acrobatics than usual. But it was, as always, all about the music. It was also all about making their music work with Miley's.

"Our favorite intro song is 'Kids of the Future,'" Joe told *m* in December 2007. "We intertwine our songs with Miley's songs."

Logistically, touring with Miley was a bigger undertaking than they were used to.

"We're doing what Kelly Clarkson and Justin Timberlake have done in the past, and we're traveling with three tour buses. One's our tour bus, the other is for the band and crew, and the third is a rolling studio. This way, we can release the next album as soon as possible. We already have new songs set to record!" Kevin told *J-14* in January 2008.

Snacks on the tour included Diet Dr Pepper, Smucker's Uncrustables PB & J sandwiches, and Dibs ice cream treats, as recorded by nosy magazine editors allowed to rummage through the bus for a story.

Their pretour rituals vary, but over the years the guys have danced around and/or prayed. In the case of Joe on the Best of Both Worlds Tour, he would do twenty push-ups "to get my energy going."

Nothing needed to be done to get the crowd's energy going—every single date was sold out and a huge outcry occurred over the hard-to-get tickets. Miley wound up apologizing to fans who had assumed their membership to her fan site guaranteed great seats.

Fans who made it into the shows were blown away, and they made sure to film as much of it as possible with their cell phones and video cameras.

"When it came to the live shows, when we saw cameras or cell phones or camera phones, it was never anything that concerned us," their manager told *Billboard* in June 2008. "We really viewed it as something that was going to expand the boys' reach."

Expanding their reach even further, the tour was filmed for Miley's 3-D movie *Hannah Montana/Miley Cyrus: Best of Both Worlds Concert Tour*. Even in limited release, the film was a huge hit and made over $65 million!

LOOK ME IN THE EYES TOUR

"I'm looking forward to the Look Me in the Eyes Tour in February. We'll play about four new songs!" Joe told *Twist*.

The next tour the guys mounted was the hastily thrown together but flawlessly executed Look Me in the Eyes Tour, from January 31 through March 22, 2008. The guys were supposed to be filming their first Disney Channel original series, but a Hollywood strike left them with a hole in their schedule.

"The good news is we get to tour instead," Kevin told *Twist* in March 2008. It wound up helping them by further promoting their *Jonas Brothers* CD and by allowing them to try out new songs from their upcoming *A Little Bit Longer* record. This time, they played thirty-nine dates and made international music headlines by signing a megabucks touring pact with Live Nation.

"We never started a tour where Joseph was born—in Arizona—so we wanted to do that this time," Kevin said of their Tucson kickoff in *Popstar!* in May 2008.

"The tour bus is like our home," Kevin told *J-14* in July

SET LIST

"Year 3000"
"Just Friends"
"Australia"
"Goodnight and Goodbye"
"Hello Beautiful"
"Take a Breath"
"Underdog"
"Shelf"
"Pushin' Me Away"
"That's Just the Way We Roll"
"Games"
"Take On Me"
"Still in Love with You"
"Hollywood"
"Burnin' Up"
"When You Look Me in the Eyes"
"Hold On"
"A Little Bit Longer"
"S.O.S."

2008. Nevertheless, "we like when we get the chance to sleep in our own beds once in a while. We like home-cooked meals, too."

For the first time, fans began to worry about the guys' exhausting, back-to-back touring. "I haven't unpacked my bag since May of last year," Kevin told *Popstar!* in July 2008. "It never ends," Nick sighed to *J-14* in its May/June 2008 issue. "We used to sit around between concerts. Now, we'll just keep on working. After every show, we have this box full of stuff to sign . . . We feed off our fans' energy."

"Things are happening so fast," Joe admitted to *J-14* in the May/June 2008 issue. "This year's been fun, but like a roller coaster. It's hard work, but we're so satisfied with where we are now."

To lighten their loads, the guys indulged in more pranks than ever before.

One prank that the guys cooked up for this tour was cold, just plain cold! "When someone's taking a shower, you freeze water—just enough so it's not frozen but super, super cold. Then you take four cups and dump it on [the guy taking] the shower, and he just freaks out. It's a good one!"

But nobody was laughing when clumsy Joe hurt himself on tour.

Joe bumped into a crate backstage after a show in Atlantic City, resulting in a few stitches in his forehead. He still has the scar. How did it happen? Well, the guys were amped after their show and goofing off, making a YouTube video, when Joe got a little carried away!

Another incident almost led to Nick being torn apart!

At their Dallas show, Nick decided to run through the crowd in an effort to get closer to his fans. It didn't work out as planned, alas. "They just crushed me," he lamented to *Teen* in Summer 2008. "We had Big Rob and two guys, Mike and Kevin, help me out, but even then it was tough."

The long spells away from their home had begun to sink in somewhat.

"We miss our friends because we don't get to see them a lot while we're out on the road," Nick told *J-14* in March 2008. Kevin concurred, saying, "We've had some painful moments in the last year. A lot of friends stab you in the back. And girlfriends break up with you or you break up with a girl. It's terrible what the road will do to you." Nick's antidote? "We're trying to keep making fun music and keep making it positive!"

"Being on the road is hard. But when we're out there performing, it's all good!" Nick told *Twist* in April 2008.

After this tour, the guys had a short break before doing some European promo dates in the summer of 2008, including some time in London, which they loved. "We started one day at the London Eye," Kevin told *People*, referring to the city's famous gigantic Ferris wheel. They later took in a production of *Les Misérables.* "It was similar to the U.S. production I was in," Nick noted, "and we enjoyed it very much." The guys also had

jonas brothers: living the dream!

When the Jonas Brothers announced a new project called *Jonas Brothers: Living the Dream*, true fans already knew what it meant. "'Livin' the Dream' is our slogan," Kevin told *J-14* in July 2008. "Every day, we pinch ourselves because this is our dream. Before we go onstage, we get together and say, 'Livin' the dream, baby!' We're living a life that people dream about, and now we can share it."

To let fans get a sneak peek inside what their lives are like during a tour—in this case, the Look Me in the Eyes Tour—the guys allowed themselves to be filmed for a reality miniseries of fifteen episodes that appeared on Disney Channel from May 16 to September 5, 2008.

The format of the show made it perfect for the guys to show off their proudly dorky personalities. It also provided equal time for each brother, since all of them narrated episodes on a rotating basis.

"Fans are getting to be a part of our life," Kevin told *Twist*. "We want our fans to see that we're just normal guys who love what we do."

Nick in particular had high hopes that *Livin' the Dream* would help their fans see that not everything is as glamorous as it looks. "I think fans will be surprised to see we're regular kids who take out the trash," he told *J-14* in July 2008.

"These boys are rock stars, but they still do chores," their dad, Kevin Sr., told *People*. "It's just that their house is a bus. You can't cut the grass, but you still have to make your bed and clean up after yourself."

Special guests who appeared on the episodes included members of their family, Selena Gomez, Cheetah Girls performer Adrienne Bailon, *Camp Rock* costars Demi Lovato and Alyson Stoner, *J.O.N.A.S.* costar Chelsea Staub, *High School Musical*'s Corbin Bleu, David Henrie from *Wizards of Waverly Place*, and other Disney and Disney Channel talent. Of all the episodes, Joe has said his favorite moment was the one involving indoor skydiving.

fun in SoHo with the old-fashioned red phone booths, teasing the palace guards, and sampling local cuisine like meat pies—though they avoided jellied eel!

While there, they opened for Avril Lavigne. Joe was dying to meet Avril and Nick called her "really pretty" in *m* in March 2008. Kevin dubbed her a "total rock star!" and said he'd love to "pick her brain."

"It was an amazing tour with Avril," Nick said in *Popstar!* in October 2008. "She's got so many hits. Some of the markets were incredible—the reaction was insane. Four weeks in, though, we were ready to come back and get into rehearsals for our own tour."

Avril returned the favor on a couple of dates of their next tour . . . Burning Up!

BURNING UP TOUR

The Jonas Brothers played forty-five shows on their Burning Up Tour, taking to the road from July 4 through August 31, 2008, featuring Demi Lovato as an opening act. "We are back in America *finally* after three months and we're so happy to be here!" Joe told *Popstar!* in October 2008 at the beginning of the tour in Detroit.

"This tour is going to be a lot of fun, and high energy," Joe told *m* in July 2008. He wasn't kidding! The massive Burning Up Tour required a quick-change room backstage, hydraulic lifts for their grand entrance, and an entire string section.

Their high-flying entrance and fiery special effects had some fans worried. "They hire a company to make sure no one gets hurt. They tell you that your feet need to be in the middle, you keep your feet in the middle," Kevin told *Popstar!* in October 2008.

"Since it is the 'Burning Up' Tour, we wanted to incorporate more things like pyrotechnics that we haven't had before," Nick revealed to *Bop* in September 2008. They also chose a long, catwalk-style stage in order to be able to mingle with fans.

"We, as a band, on this tour, really had a goal to, of course, have a good production, but more than that elevate our performance, introduce new styles of songs . . . introduce different types of music into our performance. So you might hear something and not recognize it right away, but then all of a sudden realize that it's a song we've been playing for five years now," Kevin told *Popstar!* in July 2008.

With so much invested, the pressure was palpable. "It's a really big responsibility," Kevin told *Bop* in September 2008. "We had to get more trucks and crew and people to work with, and we added some musicians, too!"

You might think they'd wilt under the pressure, but instead the guys loved the challenge—and had ways of psyching themselves up for each show. Before the show, the guys have what they describe as a "40-minute lock-down" when they hang out together, warm up vocally and dress.

Kevin told *CosmoGIRL!* in Summer 2008 that preshow he likes "to just chill out to the point where I'm not worried about anything. We set up an amazing entertainment system in our green room backstage at the venues—we even have Pro Tools so we can write and record songs."

"When we're about to perform we tell ourselves, 'We're the best band that's here.' We're normal guys when we get offstage, but it's a lot of fun to get hyped up during a show," Joe told *Tiger Beat Celebrity Spectacular!* in Summer 2008.

Their careful planning to craft an exciting show paid off—this tour attracted the biggest crowds of their careers—in the vicinity of 15,000 to 25,000 fans. They even sold out New York City's Madison Square Garden *three* times!

But at the beginning of the tour, they ran into a little problem. While the guys were on a moving bus accompanied by police escorts, some fans blocked their exit. Sensors on the bus let the driver know something was too close for comfort.

tour must-haves!

"A bathing suit is number-one priority, because you never know when you'll need it. It could be a really hot day in New York City in the winter sometimes—you never know what to expect," Joe cracked to *J-14* in its October/November 2008 issue regarding tour must-haves. More seriously, Joe told *Twist* in July 2008 that he needs sunglasses, a comfy neck pillow, and his phone while on tour. Both Nick and Kevin agreed on the phone, but Nick also has to have a computer around!

stage mishaps!

Most of the JoBros' shows are pulled off without a hitch . . . but there have been issues!

Like the time Joe hit the stage—and then literally *hit* the stage! "It was a big show so we ran and jumped on the stage and I tripped! I go face-flat onto the stage, and you hear 'BOOM!'"

Joe also told *Popstar!* in October 2006, "One time, the stage was so close to the door that you're running out of, you would run out the door and you'd be on the stage that you'd have to jump on. It was this big showcase, a lot of our fans were there, MTV, all of these big people were there. We run out and I trip onto the stage. I did a 360, too. I fell over and I fell on the ground. I was like, 'What?' All our fans gasped. I got up and did a bow, like, 'Hey, I'm here!'"

Luckily, not all of their mishaps have involved pain! "There was one time when I started freaking out because my guitar wasn't working and [then] I realized that I had not turned it up," Kevin confessed to *Tiger Beat* in September 2008. "Now, my guitar tech manages all the onstage stuff, and he'll look at me and give me a look like, 'It's on' and I'll just laugh."

"Girls were hitting the bus and lasers shot off," Joe told *J-14* in its October/November 2008 issue. "It was like *Star Wars*."

When the guys limited their meet-and-greets for the tour, some fans voiced concerns that they were changing somehow. "Some people are like, 'Oh, you've changed. You don't do meet-and-greets anymore,'" Kevin told *Teen* in Summer 2008. "But we can't do them anymore! We have to be careful where we go. We have to watch everything we do—everything is under a microscope. It's also a safety issue. But it's fun and we wouldn't change it for the world . . . In the long run, we're there for our fans, and [in] our hearts, we wish we could meet every single one of them." The guys wound up compromising, running contests for select fans to get a chance to meet them and keeping up meet-and-greets for VIPs, usually the daughters and nieces of their corporate sponsors.

One of the show's highlights had to be Nick's moving performance of "A Little Bit Longer."

"This song's for every broken heart, every lost dream, every high and low," Nick said at one of their stops. "When I'm on stage, I can't really feel or notice anything," Nick told *J-14* in the October/November 2008 issue. "It's a moment that even if I were to hurt myself, I probably won't feel it because I'm so pumped up and the adrenaline is flowing. I don't think we get nervous because we feel right at home."

"The first time you see the audience, it's the best thing ever," Kevin told *People*.

Joe, whose stage presence had become doubly

impressive and filled with confident strutting, told *Rolling Stone* he'd been inspired by frontmen like Mick Jagger of the *Rolling Stone*s and Freddie Mercury from Queen. "I heard Jagger does an hour on a treadmill before every show."

Behind the scenes, the guys were having fun with a whole host of close friends. Opener Demi Lovato raved to *Twist* in August 2008, "It's so much fun hanging out with JB. We write songs together! We stay up until the wee hours of the morning and then I have to go back to my bus."

Her BFF Selena Gomez was also spotted attending several of the shows. "Selena said, 'I can't go two months without seeing you. I'll miss you too much!'" Demi reported to *Twist* in August 2008. "So she's joining me for a little bit, but I'm not sure which days yet. I want to do a duet on stage with her, but I'm not sure if it will be on this tour!"

Of course, Selena was also around to see her secret BF, Nick!

Backstage snacks on tour were rumored to include Honey Nut Cheerios, Joe's preferred red apples with organic peanut butter, and down-home comfort foods. Nick told *Popstar!* in July 2008, "I always end up eating a turkey club or a cheeseburger!" Both Kevin and Joe are addicted to Hot Pockets, and Kev likes cereal while Joe craves Breakfast Breaks.

"Joe and I share a room when we're on tour. And we pack our own bags," Nick said to *People*. "Usually we'll drive from the venue to the next city and get to the hotel at about three in the morning. So we wake up, get out of our bunks, and then go to bed in the hotel." But, he also revealed to *CosmoGIRL!* in Summer 2008, "There are bunks on the bus, and I sleep there a lot."

In case you missed the tour, it was extensively filmed for their new movie *Jonas Brothers: The 3-D Concert Experience*. "We want our 3-D movie to be a unique and different experience for our fans!" the guys told *Twist* in August 2008.

"Since we saw the *Hannah* movie, we did a lot to enhance the 3-D aspect," Kevin told *J-14* in its October/November 2008 issue. Nick chimed in about how fun the whole shoot was, saying, "We were like, 'Wait a minute—we're shooting a 3-D movie today. How crazy is this?'"

Fandemonium!

When it comes to fans, the Jonas Brothers easily have the most enthusiastic—and sometimes craziest (in a good way)—supporters in the world! And the guys are appreciative of each and every one.

It all started out very subtly.

"We kind of get noticed a little bit more," Kevin told *Popstar!* way back in its July 2006 issue. "We walk into a mall and people start staring at us. It's a little weird, but also it's great. It's a good feeling—people know who you are!"

And, he said about the fans, "We know who you are [too]! During shows, we're always recognizing fans [who] have followed us for a while. We love all our fans and are blessed to be friends with so many of you!" Joe told *Twist* in February 2008.

"Moms are sometimes the craziest!" Joe dished to *Popstar!* in May 2008. "I think because [either] they know that they really want to get their daughters to be seen by us, or maybe *they* just want an autograph, but we've seen some moms jump in front of the bus and try to get backstage!"

When *Popstar!* asked Joe in October 2007 how the band felt about all those girls out there referring to them as their boyfriends and future husbands, Joe was quick to reply, "It's a little scary thinking about thousands of girlfriends and wives . . . but it's nice."

But probably the scariest part of having eager fans would be the rare cases of stalking.

Kevin told *Popstar!* in August 2006 that "there's girls [who] put gifts at our door. They come to our *house!* They left me a letter and they left the other boys candy. There was one line that said, 'The feeling of being near you is amazing.'"

"It's a shock to all of us," Nick said of the JoBros' crazy fans in *Rolling Stone* in its October 30, 2008, issue. "At times, it does get a little frustrating, but for the most part we have a good team that helps us keep it all together. As far as fans go: The only difficult thing is when they go in our house. That's, I mean, it's kind of odd for anybody, I think."

Once, the guys messed with some of their fans' minds in the most hilarious way! In *Popstar!* in January 2008, Joe said, "We walked up to two girls in the airport looking at *Popstar!* and they had it opened to a page with us on it. So I walked over and I was like, 'Oh, I love those magazines!' and

I walked away. They were freaked out!"

But for the most part, the guys like to pamper their fans. "Our dream is to have some of our fans win tickets to see a movie or something like that and all of a sudden, mid-movie, the screen drops and we start playing a show," Kevin told *Popstar!* in May 2008.

The things fans do to get their attention often work.

"One time, fans threw an envelope onstage," Joe said to *Tiger Beat* in September 2008. "They weighed it down with quarters so it would fly and land perfectly. It was amazing!" Kevin remembers the "cool scrapbooks. . . . One fan made a poster out of a cereal box. She was like, 'It took me forever to make!'" Nick remembers a girl they brought "up onstage to sing to her. She was freaking out, she couldn't believe it. She had written 'Jonas Brothers' on her shorts. That was funny."

"One girl from North Carolina has driven like fifteen hours to shows," Joe said to *Popstar!* in July 2006. "We call her the Jonas Sister!" He also told *Tiger Beat*, "I remember this one girl pretended to throw up to get into one of our shows."

One of the most commonly asked questions for the guys is: "Would you ever date a fan?" Turns out, the answer is yes!

Nick assured *Twist* in February 2008, "We would date a fan! We hope that any girl we date would be a fan of our music. It's nice to see the fans dancing and singing along at our shows."

Joe enjoys flirting with fans just as much as he does with any other girls he meets. "I have codes at meet-and-greets," Joe said to *Bop* in May 2008. "I give girls I like a wink sign. I also smile a lot and have a playful laugh."

Once, a fan sent the Jonas Brothers a rather sweet surprise—a little *too* sweet! "She sent me a piece of her birthday cake in the mail," Joe told *Tiger Beat* in May 2008, "and it was an ice cream cake. . . . I opened the box and it was melted and dripping in my hands. I was like, 'Wow!' And then I told her I got it, and she was like, 'Oh, did you eat it?' I was like, 'Ummm, no—it's melted!'"

While filming *Camp Rock* in Canada, the guys got a memorable dose of Jonas devotion. "Some girls showed up at the hotel," Kevin told *Bop* in August 2008. "We were three hours north of civilization, so it was kind of nuts, but it was cool."

No doubt about it—their fans have a knack for finding the guys in very odd places!

But Nick told *Popstar!* in January 2008 that no matter where they encounter fans, "it's a good feeling, kind of reassuring—like we're working, we're doing good!"

There is one place, though, where Nick does *not* like to meet fans—on planes! "I sleep all the time when I'm on planes and my mouth is, like, *wide open* while I'm sleeping. I just look totally stupid. And I'll just look around the plane and see tweens staring and taking pictures of me looking like that!"

Camp Rock

their first movie!

I n the same way he was at first a reluctant singer, Joe Jonas was not always on board to try acting. And if the opportunity arose, he hoped for a Will Ferrell–type comedy. "I could *maybe* play a serious role, but I'd want to be so funny," Joe told *Popstar!* in September 2006. "That's just my character. I love to goof around!"

But his first big movie opportunity was as the male lead in Disney Channel's *Camp Rock*, a music-driven romance patterned after the network's astonishingly successful *High School Musical* franchise.

"I sent in a video on some really ghetto camera, and Disney asked me to send it again because the film wasn't very good. They couldn't really hear my voice," Joe told *J-14* in April 2008. "For a week, I totally forgot about it, and I was like, 'There's no way I got it.' After that week, my dad and my manager sat me down in a room, and I thought I was in trouble. I was like, 'What did I do?' Everything was going through my mind. They finally told me I got the movie! I was like, 'What?' and [started] totally freaking out!"

Camp Rock was conceived as a take on Disney Channel's already successful *High School Musical*, as a film that would also be music-driven, like *HSM*, but slightly less about bursting into song and more about making musical numbers organic to the plot. The script attracted the Jonas Brothers' management immediately: When a young girl, Mitchie, finds out she gets to attend an exclusive (and expensive!) music camp, thanks to her caterer mom volunteering to work in the camp kitchen, she never dreams that rock star Shane Gray will be on the grounds, let alone that he'll overhear her singing and begin a Cinderella-like search for the girl with the magic voice! As Mitchie learns hard lessons about being honest with her friends and true to herself, Shane is reminded of just how egotistical and ungrateful he's become—and the two fall head-over-heels in love.

The brothers tend to do everything together, but in the original draft of *Camp Rock*, there were no parts for Nick and Kevin. That was soon changed, however, since Disney Channel loved the idea of including all three brothers. "They put more parts in it for Nick and Kevin to play a band," Joe told *Twist* in December 2007. The boys were written in as Shane's fed-up bandmates—but the parts were still little more than cameos. *Tiger Beat* in August 2008 questioned whether Kevin and Nick might be jealous of Joe since he was the "heartthrob" star of *Camp Rock*. So were there any bruised egos over the fact that Joe is very much the star of the movie, while his brothers play supporting roles?

Nothing could be further from the truth. "We're each other's best friends," Kevin revealed to *Tiger Beat* in August 2008, and "we were really excited for Joe," he told *Twist* in December 2007. Costar Demi Lovato confirmed that "the whole time they kept talking about how happy they were for him. They are strong. Joe could be picking his nose and his brothers would still support him."

For his part, Joe was honored by the question, even if the answer was no. "I guess it's nice to be called a

About half of the clothes they wore in *Camp Rock* were from the Jonas Brothers' own closets!

'heartthrob.' If I was put in that category, then I made my mom proud!"

"Reading the script for the first time with everyone was intimidating," Nick told *m* in December 2007 of their first cast table-read. "I wasn't too familiar with the cast, but they all turned out to be really cool!"

"I thought Nick didn't like me at first because we didn't really talk," Demi reported to *m* in May 2008. "But that's just because it takes a while for him to warm up."

Speaking of costar Demi Lovato, she admits that she came into the project with some preconceived notions. "When I first met [the Jonas Brothers], I honestly didn't think they would be that nice, because on stage they have so much confidence," Demi told *Pixie* in Summer 2008. "But they are gentlemen and some of the sweetest guys I've ever met. And they're kind of dorky in a way."

During rehearsals, Joe did a crazy dance while standing on a platform. Can you see where this is going? That's right—he took a spill! "I ran over to him and said, 'Are you okay?' He was

"But they are gentlemen and some of the sweetest guys I've ever met. And they're kind of dorky in a way."

like, 'Yeah, I'm good,' and tried to cover it up," Demi told *Pixie* in the same interview. It was a great icebreaker.

Sensing that there was some awkwardness between the leads at first, veteran director Matthew Diamond instructed Demi and Joe to "bond" by spending time together. "One night, Joe and I shared our entire life stories with each other and got to know each other extremely well," Demi revealed to *J-14* in its May/June 2008 issue.

The film's crazy schedule helped the rest of the cast to bond, also, since everyone was vulnerable to mixed-up lines and other gaffes. "We're filming day thirty-two on day one and it's really out of order. You're trying to remember what happened in the scene before," Kevin said from the set in an interview for *Fans' Choice: Stars of Summer!* 2008. Nevertheless, "It's a lot of fun . . . we're having a blast!" Kevin told *Tiger Beat* in July 2008 that he could really relate to the camp setting. "I went to camp in Pennsylvania. It's awesome. Going to camp, meeting a girl and that's all you think about the entire time—and then you [leave], and you never see her again."

Smart cookie Kevin thoroughly enjoyed playing ditzy Jason in *Camp Rock*. He told *Fans' Choice: Jonas Brothers—Living the Dream!* that his character was "a little out-there! I still have a sly know-it-all underneath the character, which is kinda funny. It's cool to play the airhead, though. I'm not usually like that."

Despite his Broadway resume, Nick told *CosmoGIRL!* in Summer 2008, "Personally, I find the acting thing to be a little more difficult than music. It's fun, but sometimes I get nervous around the cameras—I forget my lines and stuff like that."

For Nick, the best part of shooting *Camp Rock* was all the new acquaintances he made. "My favorite part of being here is being able to hang out with the cast," Nick told *Popstar!* in July 2008. "They're all about my age. I've made a couple of new friends and we're having a good time—even in school we're having a good time."

"It's fun playing this character because you're allowed to be mean," Joe told *Teen* in Summer 2008, confirming that he loved playing Shane Gray in *Camp Rock*. The main reason Joe enjoyed himself so much was because he got to pour some of himself into his character, which made his first big part a lot less intimidating. "I can connect with my character in so many ways," Joe told *J-14* in July 2008, "because Shane lives the rock-star life and is always on tour and always in front of people just like we are with the band. He's a front guy. I'm like him, except there's one big difference—he's a pretty big jerk. The fame got to his head. He was a good kid of course, but being a superstar, it got to him after a while."

"Shane tours a lot, and I can see how easy it is for things to go to your head. I'm not like him because I have great parents and they keep us grounded. We don't take advantage of everything we get," he told *Teen* in Summer 2008.

Joe's first big acting break blew away his costars, who hadn't actually expected a rock star to have any acting chops. "I was really impressed—especially with Joe," Demi told *J-14* in July 2008. "He carried a more intense role, and there were some emotional scenes, whereas Nick and Kevin were just funny the entire movie. I was shocked at their sense of humor. It was great!"

Anna Maria Perez de Tagle told *J-14* in July 2008, "Joe really carries a lot of the movie. Shane Gray is such a crazy character to play because he's a superstar with a jerky side, and Joe is totally not like that at all. And for him to pull that off is pretty good."

"Joe was phenomenal," costar Meaghan Jette Martin agreed. Meaghan, who played villainess Tess, told *J-14* in July 2008, "His character is the complete opposite of how he is in real life. Kevin's character is a total ditz, and it's hilarious because that's not Kevin at all. And Nick really shows leadership in his character."

"Joe took the role really seriously," director Matthew Diamond confirmed to *People*. "I was surprised by how rich his acting abilities are, and of course he's got enormous charisma." He also noted the genuine love and support between the three brothers—there was no jealousy rearing its ugly head in spite of Joe's plum part.

Joe was great as Shane, but not exactly perfection! For one intense scene, Joe could not remember his lines. On the third try, he screamed, "Blahhh!" to crack himself up and lighten everyone's mood. "The scene was so intense, we all needed a good laugh," Demi remembered to *Pixie* in Summer 2008.

The behind-the-scenes aspects of making *Camp Rock* were also challenging for Joe. Waking up at 5:15 a.m. every morning to prepare was a lot harder than acting, and the Canadian wilderness set was besieged by mosquitoes.

Practical jokes happened daily, but some hilarious moments couldn't be planned. "We were on the set of *Camp Rock* and Demi was jokingly punching one of the other guys in the stomach. Then Joe's like, 'Hey, punch me!' So she punched him and he farted! It was so embarrassing—they both just died laughing," Nick told *Twist* in July 2008.

Once, Demi and Joe were filming their big lovey-dovey scene by the lake when an acorn fell on Joe's head. He kept doing the scene, but Demi (and Meaghan Jette Martin, whose character was watching from a distance) cracked up! Mother Nature was *not* on his side!

Then there were all the romantic rumors . . . !

Alyson Stoner was rumored to be dating Nick, but she told *J-14* in its May/June 2008 issue, "Me and Nick? What? Are you crazy? Honestly, on the set, there are no romances. It's funny because you'd expect that and I expected that. But once we got there, we really felt like siblings."

Though Joe and Demi have always steadfastly denied they dated on the set, Demi didn't help kill rumors by gushing to *People*, "It was a dream to work with him. Any 15-year-old girl would say so." (Though one hardship was that they were banned from eating *any* chocolate while filming so it wouldn't show up in their teeth in the close-ups!)

Downtime on set was rare, but the actors made good use of it!

For one thing, Nick used his spare time to get creative. He has admitted he gets goose bumps every time he hears "This Is Me" from the film (a song so powerful that costar Meaghan Jette Martin used it to prepare herself for her most dramatic, emotional scene), and he channeled that inspiration into writing new music. In between celebrating his fifteenth birthday on the set (with sugar-free Red Bull), Nick collaborated with Demi on some songs that wound up appearing on her first album. "There were several times [Nick and I] were sitting at the piano and who knows what came out of our mouths—we just wrote it down!" Demi told *Bop* August 2008.

According to *J-14* in September 2008, when Joe found out that the girls were getting pedicures, he insisted on joining them. When they suggested he go for pink nail polish, he said, "Uh, I would . . . but tomorrow I have to shoot the scene where

I get out of the pool and you'll get to see my toes, so that would be awkward."

The bros had some bonding time as well. "Me and Joe went out on the lake and took cool pictures!" Kevin told *Twist* in April 2008.

"When we weren't filming, we played golf every day," Nick told *Twist* in the same April 2008 feature. "It was awesome!" Tennis was another favorite pastime. "Nick and the boys just started playing tennis, so I started playing with them!" Alyson Stoner told *Twist* in the May/June 2008 issue.

The actors also gathered in the Jonas Brothers' rooms to play Monopoly or for some partying!

The parties in the Jonas Brothers' villa featured dancing to '80s music like Prince, as well as Paramore, Backstreet Boys, and *NSYNC. Nick entertained everyone with his made-up dance moves set to Steve Miller Band's 1982 song "Abracadabra."

"During the slow songs, we'd pretend we were in second grade, dancing with so much space between us!" Joe told *Twist* in December 2007.

Afterward, Kevin would drive each girl back to her cabin in his golf cart to help protect them from bears. Unfortunately, he got in trouble for his gentlemanly behavior—the camp manager saw him with too many people on the cart, called it "unacceptable," and made sure Kevin had his cart privileges suspended briefly.

These get-togethers were to help alleviate boredom. "We all went out to the same restaurant every night while filming!" Nick told *Twist* in July 2008.

When the movie was finally aired across ABC platforms including Disney Channel on June 20, 2008, after months of hype, it connected with viewers in a big way—8.9 million kids tuned in!

This success has made *Camp Rock 2* very likely. In *m* in July 2008, Joe fantasized about a winter-themed *Camp Rock 2*, "or better yet, the movie should be shot in the Bahamas! I also think Shane and Mitchie's relationship will grow deeper." But in *Tiger Beat* in August 2008, Kevin insisted on "Camp Hawaii . . . I'm fine with Hawaii!"

Demi Lovato suggested that *Across the Universe* star Jim Sturgess play her crush—a little too old for you, Demi! The truth is, she'd settle for anyone to get out of kissing Joe Jonas on camera, since she has said that she thinks of the Jonases strictly as brothers!

Camp Rock was another huge hit for the Jonas Brothers, and thanks to his positive experience, Joe wants to keep up the acting sideline. "I would love to continue acting in more movies," he told *J-14* in July 2008. Good idea!

the kiss!

The biggest controversy surrounding *Camp Rock*? Its nonexistent kiss! Fans were shocked when Mitchie (Demi) and Shane (Joe) didn't smooch, mainly because interviews granted during the making of the film suggested not only that the characters *would* kiss, but that the actors definitely *had* filmed a kissing scene.

When asked if she was looking forward to kissing Joe in the movie (and if she would practice first), Demi told *Twist* in December 2007, "I don't know! The director hasn't told me yet. I wouldn't practice—it's better to go for it in the moment." But Joe told *m* in December 2007, "I'll tell you there was a kiss on the cheek."

After more scenes had been filmed, he bragged in *m*, in its January/ February 2008 issue, "Demi didn't know I was going to do it, but I jumped into the scene and kissed her. She was totally into it! Demi just popped a mint

and continued to film the scene!"

As if to confirm Joe's story, when asked in *m* in May 2008 how she and Joe had prepared for their "on-screen kiss," Demi offered, "I think we both popped a breath mint." In that magazine's following issue, Joe spoke at length about the kiss, saying, "It was funny because she didn't know about it beforehand and we had to kiss twenty-five times. It was hard because we had to jump in the scene—I jump down and I kiss her on the cheek! It had to be the perfect angle. It was so funny!"

"You will have to find out!" Demi giggled when asked in *Fans' Choice: Jonas Brothers—Living the Dream!* if the final cut contained a kiss, but she later told *Twist*, "This is the first time I am saying it—there was never a kiss! I have never kissed Joe Jonas!"

Whatever happened to kiss-and-tell?

> *"It was funny because she didn't know about it beforehand and we had to kiss twenty-five times."*

JONAS

their first TV show!

"Shooting the pilot was the greatest experience ever."

"When the subject first came up, we told them we didn't want the show to be cheesy."

JONAS, the sitcom starring the Jonas Brothers that debuted in spring 2009, was a constant source of intrigue, excitement, and disappointment for hard-core fans, who had anxiously awaited its debut for almost two years!

Before any fans knew that a Jonas Brothers TV show was even a possibility, the boys were presented with the idea, loved the original concept (which featured them as undercover spies), and filmed a pilot in the summer of 2007. The original pilot was full of slapstick humor and the guys goofing off as mini James Bonds—perfect since Nick's ringtone was, at one time, the James Bond theme song. They'd even done kung fu training for the show. Only a few snippets of that original pilot have been leaked on YouTube.

"Shooting the pilot was the greatest experience ever," Joe told *Life Story* in Winter 2008. "The single-camera approach is exactly what we wanted. Having a laughtrack is great, but this gives people the opportunity to laugh for themselves."

"When the subject first came up, we told them we didn't want the show to be cheesy," Kevin told *Life Story* in Winter 2008. "We wanted there to be stunts and for the episodes to be action-packed."

The female lead was *Minutemen*'s Chelsea Staub, who

got the confirmation call from Kevin Jonas himself that she had been chosen.

"They are all so amazing," Chelsea told *m*, in its January/February 2008 issue, speaking of her time with the guys while shooting *JONAS*. "Kevin brings me coffee to the set in the morning. Oh! And once I was having a snack attack and they went and got me Pinkberry frozen yogurt. The show is going to be really cool. The guys play a band who have a double life as spies. I'm a reporter for a teen magazine who's out to uncover their secret."

"It's going to be a fun show," Chelsea told *J-14* in August 2008. The series idea seemed to have shifted a little bit by then. "It's going to be like *The Monkees* and a little bit of *Mr. & Mrs. Smith*. There's going to be fun action sequences and still be a sitcom. It's the first time a girl is thrown into the mix with all three boys. It's not just a romance with one of them. It's a spy team with three guys and a girl. Adding a female into the mix makes it a little different."

In *Popstar!* in November 2007, Kevin said, "With the script, they're very open with us. If we were like, 'I would never, ever say that line,' you know, they'd change it." Nick wanted fans to know, "The characters are us, so they kind of have to fit our personalities. We got time to meet the writers so they got to know who we are. It was cool!"

"Shows like *The Suite Life of Zack & Cody* are restricted to their sets," Nick told *Life Story* in Winter 2008. "With our show, we can build different sets every day. We could have a big warehouse and they would build a school in it one day. Then the next day, they would knock it down and build an evil lair. It's just unbelievable."

"The characters are us, so they kind of have to fit our personalities. We got time to meet the writers so they got to know who we are. It was cool!"

The show went from being compared to The Monkees *to* Flight of the Conchords.

"After our [Marvelous Party] tour we're going straight into shooting!" Nick told *Twist* in an interview that appeared in December 2007. But it wasn't meant to be—the writers' strike put the show on hold, so the boys instead mounted their Look Me in the Eyes Tour . . . and then the show's concept began to morph behind the scenes.

By the time the boys did an interview with *Billboard* in June 2008, the show was being called a sitcom about "world-beating rock stars who also go to high school," and *J.O.N.A.S.*, an acronym for Junior Operatives Networking As Spies, was a tentative title.

Quick as a flash, Joe told *Twist* in its October/November 2008 issue, "The show's changed a bit. Now, it's going to be more about everyday life rather than us being spies." It also lost the periods and became *JONAS*, named after the street on which the Jonases live in the show.

The show went from being compared to *The Monkees* to *Flight of the Conchords*.

In *Twist* in July 2008, Nick said his character on the revised series was supposed to be dating Chelsea Staub—a major burn since, in real life, she was rumored to be dating Joe! "I date her in the show, so Joe's beat!" Nick said mischievously.

The show's scope changed, too—it went from having no budget to being a big-budget vehicle for an established group.

"It will be weird for us, I think, being in one place for many weeks," Joe told *Billboard*. But once they finished their Burning Up Tour, the guys parked in L.A. and began filming episodes in September 2008.

As for what to expect from the show, the guys told Ryan Seacrest, "We can just pick up the guitar and break into song—in really funny situations."

73

JoBro Profile

Nick!

NICK FACTS!

BORN: September 16, 1992, in Dallas, Texas

HEIGHT: 5'6"

WEIGHT: 115 lbs.

BOXERS OR BRIEFS: Boxer-briefs

FAVE FOODS: Cheerios, SweeTarts, steak, McDonald's two-cheeseburger meal with three-piece Chicken Selects

CHOICE MUSIC: Elvis Costello, Hellogoodbye, Fall Out Boy, Daft Punk

PERSONAL THEME SONGS: Elvis Costello's "(I Don't Want to Go to) Chelsea" and Johnny Cash's "Give My Love to Rose." (He even wanted to do an album cover of Cash tunes: *Jonas Brothers Pay Tribute to the Man in Black*.)

ROLE MODELS: Elvis Costello, The Beatles, Derek Jeter

CELEBRITY LOOK-ALIKE: Nick told *Teen* Summer 2008 that people tell him he looks like Mark Wahlberg

CELEBRITY CRUSHES: Camilla Belle: "While we were on tour in Boston, we saw the movie *10,000 B.C.* I definitely fell in love when I saw that, because she is absolutely gorgeous." (Joe later started dating Camilla...doh!) On the red carpet at the 2006 *Nickelodeon Kids' Choice Awards*, Kevin said they were "trying to hook Nick up with Emma Roberts or Jamie Lynn Spears tonight." Nick said, "Or both!" But as Joe pointed out, "We've never even met them, so we're hoping we can work some magic!"

SPORTS TEAMS: The New York Yankees and the Dallas Cowboys

PREFERRED SPORTS: Golf and baseball

MUST-SEE TV: *Lost* and *SportsCenter*

CLASSIC MOVIES: *Finding Neverland*

CHILDHOOD BOOK: *Civil War on Sunday* by Mary Pope Osborne, from the Magic Tree House series

FUN FLASHBACK: "I had this Batman costume that I was really fond of," Nick told *Twist* October/November 2008 of a prized possession from his childhood. "It was awesome. I'd run around in my backyard and be Batman!"

A FEW OF HIS FAVORITE THINGS: For a *People* special, Nick listed his favorite things as his Gibson ES-345 guitar, his Miu Miu tie, his bandanna, his green Converse (interestingly, Selena Gomez is a huge Converse fan!), sugar-free Red Bull, his vintage Elvis Costello T-shirt (yes, the same one Selena was photographed wearing, too!) and his custom-made guitar strap.

Stars the Jonas Brothers have met who have impressed Nick the most were Barry Gibb of the Bee Gees, Heather Locklear, and Steve Jobs.

His eyes are supersensitive to the sun.

According to Kevin, Nick's closets are color-coordinated!

His favorite roller coasters are the Tower of Terror, Rock 'n' Roller Coaster, and Expedition Everest, all at Walt Disney World!

Nick loves Diet Coke and has been known to drink up to four a day.

Mandy Van Duyne (the girl for whom their first single, "Mandy," was named and a close family friend) says the one word for Nick is "protective."

Nick's feet are very ticklish.

THE LITTLE LEADER!

"Nicholas has always been older than he was," his father Kevin told Rolling Stone.

Nick is significantly younger than Joe and Kevin, but everyone knows he's the leader of the group. "Even though we have a younger brother [Frankie], I'm considered the baby," Nick confessed to *Bop* in March 2007. "But I'm more adult than Kevin and Joe." This is a fact, but it's one the brothers occasionally try to torpedo! "They treat me like the baby because I'm the leader," Nick boldly told *Popstar!* in September 2006. The guys know Nick is their boss, so they try to put him in his place by reminding him he's actually younger . . . but it doesn't work! "I won't beat them up, but I'll know what to say."

"Nick's the most responsible. He's the boss. We're saying Nick will run for president—Nick J in '38!" Kevin told *Twist* in its May/June 2008 issue. (Nick will actually be old enough in the election year of 2028!)

Part of his ability to take control of situations and inspire leadership comes from his childhood experience of being bullied. "Nobody understood me in school," Nick wrote in *m* in July 2006 in response to a reader's question about bullying. "But now when I look back at it I just think it's funny! Don't let their words get to you. People can be stupid, and that's the truth!" Overcoming the feeling of powerlessness actually helped empower Nick.

He also had to learn how to realign people's opinions of him since his devotion to acting and singing made him something of an outcast at school. "I remember a time when I felt like I didn't fit in," Nick said, opening up to *Tiger Beat* in September 2008. "When I was younger and acting in Broadway shows, some people my age didn't understand what I was doing. They didn't quite get it, and that would frustrate me. It was very hard to talk to my friends about anything when they didn't understand the one thing I did most."

SHY GUY?

Nick is considered the "shy" Jonas Brother because he is sometimes quiet during interviews. But that simply is not the case! He's actually very outgoing. "I heard that everyone was saying I am shy. Not true!" he told *Twist* forcefully in its May/June 2007 issue. "I actually do have a sense of humor. No one really knows!"

"People think Nick's shy, but he's just an old soul," close pal Demi Lovato told *Twist* in July 2008. "I always joke and say he's the oldest person I know. He's got the most witty, smart sense of humor! When you're around him, everyone laughs. It's great!"

"Nick's not as shy as everyone thinks!" Joe told *Twist* in September 2008. Nick agreed, saying, "I show my funny side in YouTube videos like 'The Nick J Show.' We were in the back lounge of our bus when we filmed it and, I don't know, I just kind of went out of character!"

One of the main reasons he's mistakenly considered to be shy is that he's not overly outgoing around people he doesn't know well. "I don't like talking on the phone that much," he told *Twist* in April 2008. And he almost never takes the lead in group interviews.

Rather than shy, think of Nick as being thoughtful and focused. "I really like to find time to be by myself and just relax, like even if it's just sitting down to watch TV for a little while," Nick told *Twist* in March 2008. "I think for any guy it's important to find time to be by yourself, just to kick back."

Maybe the only thing he's shy about is his dancing! Cody Linley told *Twist* in August 2008, "I bonded with Nick Jonas at the DC Games party because everyone was dancing and I said, 'Yeah, I can't dance.' And he said, 'I know, me neither!' We were like, 'There's lots of people here and everyone's going to be watching!'" Well, Cody later did pretty well on *Dancing with the Stars*, so maybe there's hope for Nick yet!

NICK . . . WILD MAN?

He may be devoted to his art, but Nick's as fun-loving as the next Jonas! He likes parties if he knows and is comfortable with the attendees. "I don't hang with people that make me feel awkward," Nick told *m* in August 2008. His motto is "Try to avoid situations that make you feel weird in any way."

At parties, Nick told *People* he likes "to play deejay. I'll play a lot of older songs like Michael Jackson and then some slower jams like Chicago. I work the lights, too."

That sense of fun translates into some serious pranksterism! "I'm good at pulling pranks," Joe told *Twist* in its October/November 2008 issue, "but Nick's the *mastermind* behind them! He'll come up with a good idea and then he'll think of a sneaky way to pull it off."

HE'S THE FOCUS OF THIS GROUP

Nick gets ready quickly, and is known for taking "two-minute showers." He's a man on a mission who never dawdles.

"Nicholas has always been so focused," his mother Denise told *m* in May 2007. "When he was eight, we took a family vacation, and Nick chose not to go so he wouldn't miss work! That year, he worked forty hours a week, went to school full time, and was the star soccer player on a town league!"

Even Nick himself used the words "focused, fun, and smart" in *Twist* in July 2008 to describe who he is.

Nick's so dedicated to his craft, he does everything he can to capture any potentially usable ideas. He writes songs on the fly, and in *Rolling Stone*'s October 30, 2008, issue, he said, "I keep a lot of stuff on the computer, but I also do it on my phone. For me, typing on my computer is more of a convenient way sometimes to do things, because I don't have much time.

"Try to avoid situations that make you feel weird in any way."

I have to put it down quickly. Then, when we're in the studio, I can send the lyrics off to the brothers."

"I'm not really into the whole luck thing. I just do my best and try to be as good as I can be at an instrument, my voice, or performing, and hope it will take me to the next level," he said to *J-14* in March 2008.

So if you ever thought Nick Jonas became famous due to luck, think again—it was mostly thanks to his hard work and focus, focus, focus!

MR. SOFTIE

Despite his serious demeanor, people who know Nick know he's a teddy bear—and always has been!

His mom said, "Nick would take our DustBuster, turn it upside down, and push it around because he loved the way it sounded. He would look up at us and smile with his little binky in his mouth . . . Nick would never get into trouble. He wasn't mischievous."

When asked about the nicest thing he's ever done for someone, Nick couldn't narrow it down to one particular act, for a very touching reason. "I like to spread it out," Nick said to *J-14* in December 2007. "I usually don't do one huge thing that's really nice. I like to spread little gifts out here and there."

The ultimate way to tell how kind and how real Nick is, is in his attitude toward his fans . . . no star alive appreciates their fans more than Nick J and his brothers! "When we meet fans and they tell us they're inspired by our songs, I feel blessed!" Nick told *Twist* in July 2008.

how to be famous!

Nick told *Tiger Beat Celebrity Spectacular!* in Summer 2008, "Practice as hard as you can. If you're a songwriter, try to write as many of your own songs as you can. When you get to a point where you're starting to see success, it's really important to stay humble."

"Talent has so much to do with it," Kevin told *J-14* in March 2008. "But, of course, meeting the right people and falling in the right situation is so much a part of it. You learn that, in the business, it's not about how good you are. It's about the people you know. . . . We are lucky enough to have the most amazing team behind us."

Joe!

JOE FACTS!

BORN: August 15, 1989, in Casa Grande, Arizona

HEIGHT: 5′8″

WEIGHT: 140 lbs.

BOXERS OR BRIEFS: Briefs

FAVE FOODS: Red apples with organic peanut butter

CHOICE MUSIC: Switchfoot and Jonny Lang

ROLE MODELS: Mick Jagger and Freddie Mercury

CELEBRITY LOOK-ALIKE: Robert Carmine of Rooney

CELEBRITY CRUSHES: Joe's celebrity crush is Jessica Alba—this is well known to his fans, who occasionally carry signs saying "I'm Jessica Alba!" so he'll do a double take from the stage. When he was at the Teen Choice Awards, Joe introduced himself to the star. She almost didn't know who he was, then said, "I'm supposed to get an autograph from you guys." It was for her maid's daughter.

PREFERRED SPORTS: Baseball

MUST-SEE TV: *Heroes* and *Lost*

CLASSIC MOVIES: All from the James Bond series, plus he was terrified by *The Ring*. He told *Twist* in its October/November 2008 issue, "I watched it with a girl once and I had to try to act tough and be the man. She was scared, so I put my arm around her. But every now and then, I jumped up out of my seat—I'm pretty sure she noticed, too!"

CHILDHOOD BOOK: *Are You My Mother?* by P. D. Eastman

FUN FLASHBACK: Joe loved his G.I. Joe as a kid (maybe it was the name?)

FRUSTRATING FLAWS: First of all, clumsiness! Joe, who has fallen onstage several times, told *Bop* in December 2006, "I'll put on a jacket and accidentally slap someone in the face!" Also, Joe is not known for his promptness. Kevin told *Bop* in its June/July 2006 issue that "Joseph, by far," was the tardiest of the three. "Kevin gets two wake-up calls—one for him to wake up, and one for him to wake me up!" Joe confirmed.

LUCKY CHARMS: "I have a ring and special socks that I always wear," Joe admitted to *J-14* in March 2008. "My socks are very colorful and really comfortable."

A FEW OF HIS FAVORITE THINGS: Joe's favorite things are his Ray-Bans (he's got a case of the sunglasses in various colors), his Kiehl's products (especially the lip balm and Facial Fuel), his Casio keytar, his custom VOS Les Paul guitar, his DVD of *Juno* ("It's a great real-life teen movie"), and his Superga sneakers. Joe also loves his iPhone. "It's always nearby," he told *People*.

Joe never got his driver's license, at least as of November 2007, when he told *Tiger Beat*, "That's the most rock star thing to do, never get your license."

Mandy Van Duyne (of "Mandy" fame) used to date Joe, so she knows him well. She says the one word for Joe is "caring."

He's the most starstruck JoBro! "When we meet really famous celebrities, I turn into the shy one!" Joe told *Twist* in September 2008.

Joe knows the secret to being a star with die-hard fans. He told *Tiger Beat Celebrity Spectacular!* in Summer 2008, "You have to be nice. If you're a jerk nobody wants to meet you or be your friend."

Joe loves when people have accents, and enjoys imitating them.

81

PET PROJECT!

Joe is an animal lover—he was devastated when his dog Cocoa, a black Lhasapoo (a Lhasa Apso/poodle mix), died at the ripe old age of thirteen. "When my dog passed away, it was really tough," he told *Bop* in May 2008. "We were in Toronto filming . . . after a big shot, my parents told me. I was so bummed out. I'm okay now. He was my dog since the beginning. I have a picture of him and me in my wallet." In *m*'s January/February 2008 issue, Joe admitted, "He was my dog, my puppy." He had even picked Cocoa out as a five-year-old from an animal-rescue organization. Denise had been against the idea (parents realize how much hard work raising pets can be . . . and who usually ends up doing the work! Hint: it's not the kids), but she told *m*, "That puppy won me over. His name was Coal, but I said, 'Coal is something Santa puts in your stocking if you're bad, so we'll call you Cocoa because you are dark and sweet!'"

Over the years, Cocoa got into his share of mischief. While the boys were filming the "Year 3000" video, Cocoa was being looked after by family friends. He somehow escaped, and was found by some helpful policemen.

When they began touring, Cocoa went to live with the Jonases' grandparents in Arizona, which is where he passed away. "Maybe I'll get another dog one day," Joe told *m*, admitting that he'd cried over the news of Cocoa's passing. "After I found out, I immediately called Demi and was like, 'Can you talk?' She opened the door to her hotel room and gave me the biggest hug. I was so upset," Joe said in *m* in July 2008.

By the October 2008 issue of *Bop*, Joe was making plans for a new pet. "I'd really like to get [another] dog. I want one that's younger so it can grow up and be my buddy. I want a big dog because I know it can take care of me and I can take care of it."

On the subject of animals, Joe told *Tiger Beat Celebrity Spectacular!* in Fall 2008 that if he could be any animal, he would be a kangaroo. "You can hop around all over the place. You can get around faster, and if anyone messes with you, you can just kickbox them."

LATE BLOOMER!

Growing up, Joe remembers himself as "a weird kid. I used to think it was cool to go to bed and pretend to fall asleep and then get up and change into my school clothes for the next day and sleep in them. I don't know why! I guess I wanted to be prepared for the next morning."

Joe was also Barney's #1 fan. He told *People*, "I had a Barney glow-in-the-dark T-shirt and I would go into my closet in my room in the middle of the afternoon and stare at the shirt." He also traded Pokémon cards.

"Joe is the most outgoing, but when he was young, he was very quiet," his mom, Denise, recalled in *m* in May 2007. He was helpful, too. "When his youngest brother Frankie was born, Joe was so excited. The first night home from the hospital, he awoke to help me with each feeding and diaper change! I could not have made it through the night without him!"

"I was always trying to fit in with the cool crowd," proud mama's boy Joe remembered in *m* in August 2008. "Everyone goes through peer pressure like that. It's okay to be who you are. Hang out with the friends you're comfortable with. Don't be someone you're not."

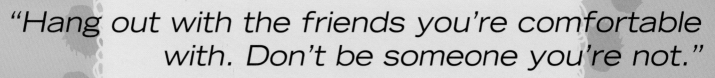

"Hang out with the friends you're comfortable with. Don't be someone you're not."

A GIRL-CRAZY GUY!

Joe told *Twist* in September 2008 he was not confident, but rather a sneaky grade-schooler when it came to girls! "I used to write notes to my crush. Like maybe two days a week, I'd write ones like, 'What's up, girl?' Then, I'd put it in her locker. I'd slip it through those little holes in the locker, and I wouldn't sign my name so she didn't know who it was from!"

Denise told *J-14* in its May/June 2008 issue that when he was older, Joe became quite the little lover boy. "Joseph brought this girl he liked a pretty little stone that said something on it and put it in a heart box and gave it to her. She rejected him!"

He was so interested in girls it was the main reason he started performing, once he witnessed how popular his brothers were getting with the ladies "Seeing the reactions they got from the girls, I was like, 'Maybe I *should* try and sing,'" Joe admitted in *CosmoGIRL!* in Summer 2008. "And then I fell in love with it."

He may have gotten over his reluctance to sing, but he's never gotten over being girl-crazy—he's the Jonas all three brothers call the biggest flirt!

MR. ENERGY!

Joe has always loved making home movies, which brings out his personality. He often films himself goofing off, leading to a larger-than-life presence that's gotten him teased by his brothers. They say he's always "on."

"They say I'm like the loudest person on the phone ever," Joe told *Popstar!* in September 2006. "I'm like, 'Hey, how's it going?!' and they're always like, 'Joe, shut up!' I'm like, 'I can't help it—we're all in a bus together!'"

Joe told *Bop* he'd be a comedian if he weren't a rock star. "I've always loved to make people laugh."

Part of Joe's high energy comes from being superfit. "I like working out—especially running," Joe said in *Twist*'s October/November 2006 issue. He doesn't just work out, he works out *every day*, benchpressing up to 165 pounds. He finds that it

"It's cool when someone says something like, 'Your triceps look huge!'"

builds his confidence and, of course, makes his body stronger for the rigors of performing. "It's cool when someone says something like, 'Your triceps look huge!'" he told *People*.

BIG-HEARTED JOE!

For Joe's nineteenth birthday, he went the opposite route of most teen stars—he didn't have it in Vegas or at a club. Instead, as he told *Twist* in its October/November 2008 issue, "We hung out at our house and had a bonfire party for my birthday. A bunch of my friends came."

This kind of story reveals how down-to-earth Joe is—in fact, despite his flashy onstage persona, he's always been the opposite of a rock star in his personal behavior.

"Joe is just quiet, very sweet," Denise told *J-14* in its May/June 2008 issue. "But he has a mischievous side. When he was little, he had an adorable face, big brown eyes, and puffy hair—straight mushroom. Joseph was very attached to his Barney bank, and I was like, we have to get rid of this thing. I had my friend bring it to the trash and Joe saw her. He said, 'Why do you have my Barney?'"

The one time Joe really got into trouble growing up, he was so young he had no idea why what he'd done was so bad. "Joseph found pills and passed them out to neighborhood kids. He said they were candy! We had to call poison control. The kids' moms were so upset." Thankfully, "No one swallowed them. They were aspirin."

maya: the "jonas sister"

Unbeknownst to even some hard-core Jonas fans, the boys also have a sister . . . sort of! Maya Kibbel is considered to be like a sister to the guys—frequently traveling with them—because the Jonas family has taken care of her and her mom ever since her father died suddenly when she was a baby. "Growing up with the Jonas family was a lot of fun!" she wrote in the *Tiger Beat Celebrity Spectacular!* Summer 2008 issue. "Since Nick was closest to my age, I spent the most time with him. He is my best friend and always has my back." As children, Maya and Nick would play in the Jonases' basement and put on little skits for the family to see. And in case you were wondering if she might be jealous of their fame, nothing could be further from the truth! "I am so happy for the guys! They have worked really hard and deserve this so much!"

JoBro Profile

Kevin!

BORN: **November 5, 1987, in Teaneck, New Jersey**

HEIGHT: **5'8"**

WEIGHT: **135 lbs.**

BOXERS OR BRIEFS: **Boxer-briefs**

FAVE FOODS: **Sushi and Thai food, Cocoa Puffs, Butterfingers**

CHOICE MUSIC: **Oasis, My Chemical Romance, and John Mayer**

ROLE MODEL: **James Dean**

CELEBRITY LOOK-ALIKE: **Drake Bell**

PREFERRED SPORT: **Baseball**

HOT HOBBIES: **Painting, driving (although due to his busy schedule, the black Jeep Commander Kevin leased a couple of years ago only took on 2,000 miles in its first eighteen months!)**

MUST-SEE TV: *Heroes* and *Lost*

CHILDHOOD BOOKS: **Anything by Shakespeare**

FUN FLASHBACK: **Kevin's after-school job was mowing lawns.**

FRUSTRATING FLAWS: **He tends to be a li'l bit bossy! "I loved being the oldest because I bossed my brothers around!" Kevin told** *Twist* **in its October/November 2006 issue.**

HIDDEN TALENTS: **Kevin can burp on command and is double-jointed.**

A FEW OF HIS FAVORITE THINGS: **Kevin's fave things in the world are his custom Gibson Les Paul guitar (he has several different white guitars), Pinkberry, his vintage suspenders, his collection of scarves, his Louis Vuitton messenger bag, his Iron Army jeans, and those vintage black buckle shoes we always see him wearing ("When I first got them, I freaked out," he told** *People.* **"I wear them all the time still.").**

"Whenever I play a show, I have to have *my* guitar," Kevin told *J-14* in March 2008. "It's one of those things. It fits my hands perfectly and no one else's. It's like made for me."

Kevin told *Popstar!* that if his life were a TV show, it would be *Boy Meets World!*

He was a varsity bowler in high school.

Kev is ticklish only on his right side.

Mandy Van Duyne says the one word for Kevin is "encourager."

According to *J-14* in July 2008, Kevin once pranked his favorite teacher! His teacher had just bought a new house, and Kevin told him the realtor called to say the roof had collapsed! He then gave the poor guy a number to call . . . and it was Kevin's own cell. "April fool!" Kevin said when he called. Devious!

Kevin hates fruit, especially bananas. "Even the smell of a banana makes me nauseous," he told *Tiger Beat* in May 2007.

87

FROM OUTCAST TO SOCIAL BUTTERFLY!

"I was a total nerd in school!" Kevin remembered to *Twist* in September 2008. "I had large ears—I had to grow into them!" Being different led to lots of teasing, and it probably shaped how Kevin turned out as an adult.

"In school, there were lots of bullies. They used to make fun of me and beat me up," Kevin confessed to *m* in September 2008. He had earlier said to *m*, in May 2007, "I used to get picked on a lot, and I'm terrible at comebacks. I handled it by finding a few good friends and hanging out with them. So when kids started to make fun of me or tried to push me around, my friends were there to stand up for me."

Unfortunately, Kevin did sometimes take his frustrations out on little bro Joe. "Kevin talked nonstop," mom Denise told *J-14* in its May/June 2007 issue. "He is full of personality and full of life, a happy and joyful kid. Kevin put Joseph up to stuff, and I'm just finding out now. Kevin was so convincing, and we would always believe what Kevin said. He would blame Joseph."

In the end, Kevin survived the bullying and eventually came to see Joe as one of his best friends in the world, not as a punching bag or scapegoat. Once he had built up his confidence thanks to his closest friends and his supportive brothers, Kevin became incredibly outgoing and warm (he's *always* on his phone with friends), losing his fear of being teased and tormented.

"I'm a people person, and I try to make everyone feel comfortable," Kevin told *J-14* in December 2007.

IF HE HADN'T BECOME A ROCK STAR . . .

Kevin almost became a movie star instead of a musical sensation! In 1994, he tried out for a remake of the classic film *Miracle on 34th Street*. "It was a whole big thing," he recalled for *CosmoGIRL!* in Summer 2008. "They thought about going with a boy in the lead role . . . but they ended up sticking with a girl in the end."

Instead, he'll make his big-screen acting debut alongside

all three of his brothers in the outrageous Farrelly Brothers comedy *Walter the Farting Dog* in late 2010.

In addition to acting, Kevin's also been motivated by charitable efforts—perhaps he would have made a good missionary or relief worker in an impoverished area? "Kevin has been involved in many wonderful charity efforts," Denise told *m* in May 2007. "He has traveled several times to Mexico and Indonesia to help build hospitals, schools, and churches. He has lived among, fed, played with, and sung to orphans in many countries. He has a precious heart!"

But Kevin is pretty sporty, too. He learned how to pole-vault in school. He told *Bop* in February 2007 that he liked it so much he went to pole-vaulting camp to help take his mind off of a painful breakup! Kevin might have been a pro athlete or an Olympian if he'd stuck with it.

Finally, what do you think about Kevin as a cowboy? It's not as crazy as it sounds—he went to rodeos when he was a kid in Texas and at age nine, he won a halftime show where he had to get the ribbon off a calf. "I always wanted to be a cowboy growing up," Kevin said to *Twist* in its October/November 2008 issue. "I even had the ultimate outfit. I had the spurs and boots and the bolero hat!"

Luckily, Kevin followed his heart and went into singing . . . but he definitely had backup plans!

PUBLICITY, PLEASE!

Kevin is very private, and he reacted with shock that fans who've figured out where the family lives think it's a great idea to go sightseeing . . . at the boys' house! "It's amazing, but kind of odd and creepy. Random people will stop by our house now," he complained to *J-14* in August 2008.

Despite his aversion to surprise guests, Kevin is like the group's built-in publicist. In the summer of 2008, after they toured Europe, Kevin made sure to ask the band's record-label publicist to set up phone interviews with all the top teen magazines just to be sure the editors had all the quotes they needed. But although he likes to give good interviews to magazines, he's wise enough to know that gossip isn't good for anyone—Kevin told *Teen* in Summer 2008 that if he heard some juicy gossip, he'd most likely tell "the person it's about."

frankie

frankie: the "bonus" jonas!

Ever since the Jonas Brothers began making an impact as a group, their kid brother, Frankie, has captivated their fans with his impish sense of humor and cute presence. *Popstar!* dubbed him "the Bonus Jonas" in its November 2006 issue, and he's been a star in his own right ever since.

"He acts older than us," Joe revealed to *Popstar!* in September 2006. "He says, 'Joe teaches me all the bad stuff!' I did *not* say that to him. Like, 'Oh, great . . . thanks, Frankie!'"

He's not only popular with fans, but also with his brothers' famous pals. Their *Camp Rock* costar Alyson Stoner told *J-14* in July 2008 that Frankie is her fave Jonas brother! "He just likes to enjoy life, and he's such a cool, slick dude." Meaghan Jette Martin, also from the movie, agreed, saying, "Frankie's my favorite, too. He's my hero. I want to be like Frankie when I grow up. He's a charmer. He's hilarious."

"Frankie is so funny because he's such a mini diva," Joe told *Tiger Beat* in June 2008. "He's very talented. He's very smart." Kevin added, "In a word, he's awesome." Even Nick, who's always referred to as the "president" of the JoBros, said, "When he's on the road with us, he's like 'the man'!"

With so many built-in fans, will Frankie one day join his brothers in the band?

As early as *Popstar!*'s January 2006 issue, Frankie was making his move. Kevin reported, "He told us, 'I'm going to make my own band!' But yesterday he decided, 'I'm going to play drums with my brothers—but *only* on a couple songs I like!'"

In *m* in June 2007, the guys said, "We'd love to have Frankie in JB, but he doesn't want to be! He wants his own band. BUT, we may be doing another project with Frankie in the very near future!"

"One day, he might join the band, but he's got his own band that he's excited about right now," Joe told *J-14* in July 2008.

Yep, he's got a band—they've been called Hollywood Shakeup, RockSlap, and Webline over the years. Frankie, who actually shared a bunk bed with Nick until recently, believes that by the time his band is famous, his older brothers will be opening for *him*!

What's he like in person? He's got a mischievous sense of humor and can sometimes be in his own little world. Frankie told *People* he can't live without TV because "it mesmerizes me."

But the tween has already discovered girls!

Nick confessed *to Tiger Beat* in its January/February 2008 issue, "I had a problem with my little brother, Frankie. I was saying that I thought [Miley Cyrus] was cute, and [he] started to beat me up!"

"We always video chat with all our friends instead of talking on the phone. Frankie video chats. Oh, man, he and Noah, Miley's little sister . . . they video chat all the time. It's actually kind of funny," Kevin told *J-14* in February 2008. During the Best of Both Worlds Tour, he said, "Frankie has a little buddy to hang along with on tour. They cause mayhem. She's a little firecracker, too. It's awesome when they're together."

take the jonas compatibility quiz!

nick

START

I love writing!

I hate gossip!

I fall in love easily!

I'm extremely outgoing!

I'm sometimes called "shy"

My life is an open book!

A smart guy is a hot guy!

I'm not competitive by nature!

I'm full of energy!

I'm the least jealous person ever!

just friends

more than friends

true love

joe

START
Personality is everything!

F · T

I love live theater!

I'm the funniest person I know!

T · F

I don't like exotic foods on a dinner date!

F · T

I have an accent other than American!

I think doing impressions of people is kinda mean!

T · F

I don't mind being made fun of!

F · T

I hate when I'm the center of attention!

I'm blonde!

F · T

My ideal date is just hanging out!

F · T

just friends

more than friends

true love

kevin

START
I used to be a social misfit!

F · T

I'm more into movies than music!

I don't understand boys!

F · T

I'm old-fashioned!

F · T

What people think of me is not important!

I haven't had too many huge crushes!

F · T

I'm a leader...not a follower!

I'm easy to get along with!

F · T

I'm a very private person!

F · T

I only watch TV for a couple of fave shows!

F · T

just friends

more than friends

true love

93

Jonas Brothers Photo Gallery!

kevin

joe

kevin

jonas brothers

nick

kevin

jonas brothers

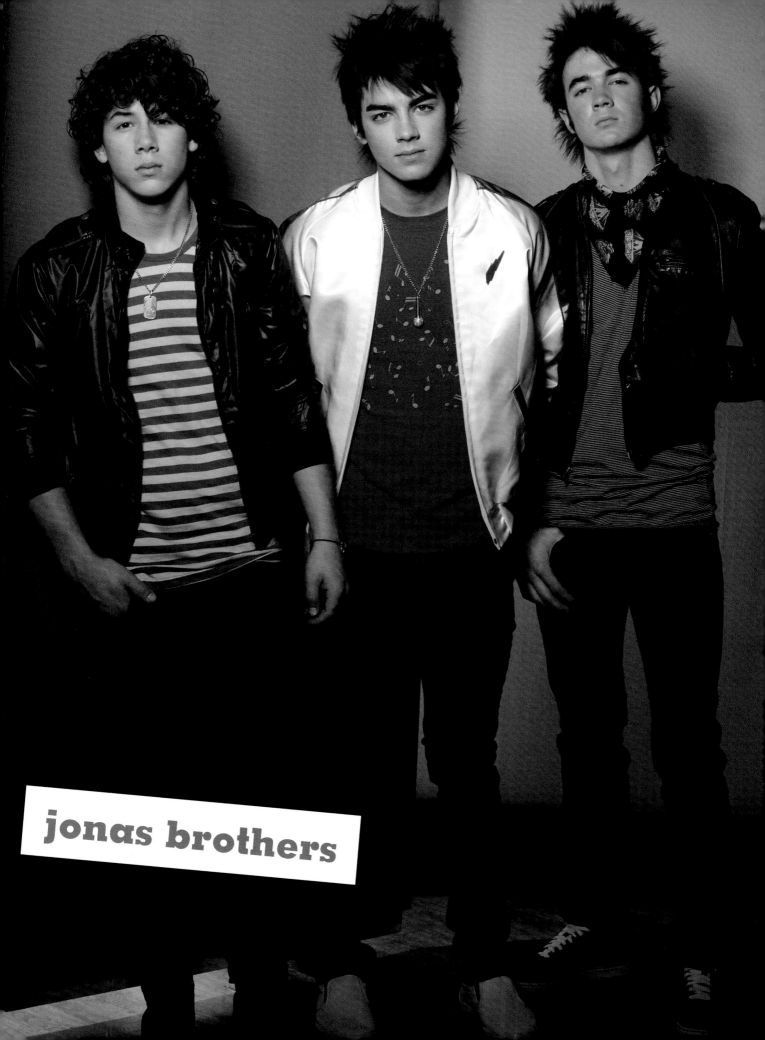

jonas brothers

nick

jonas brothers

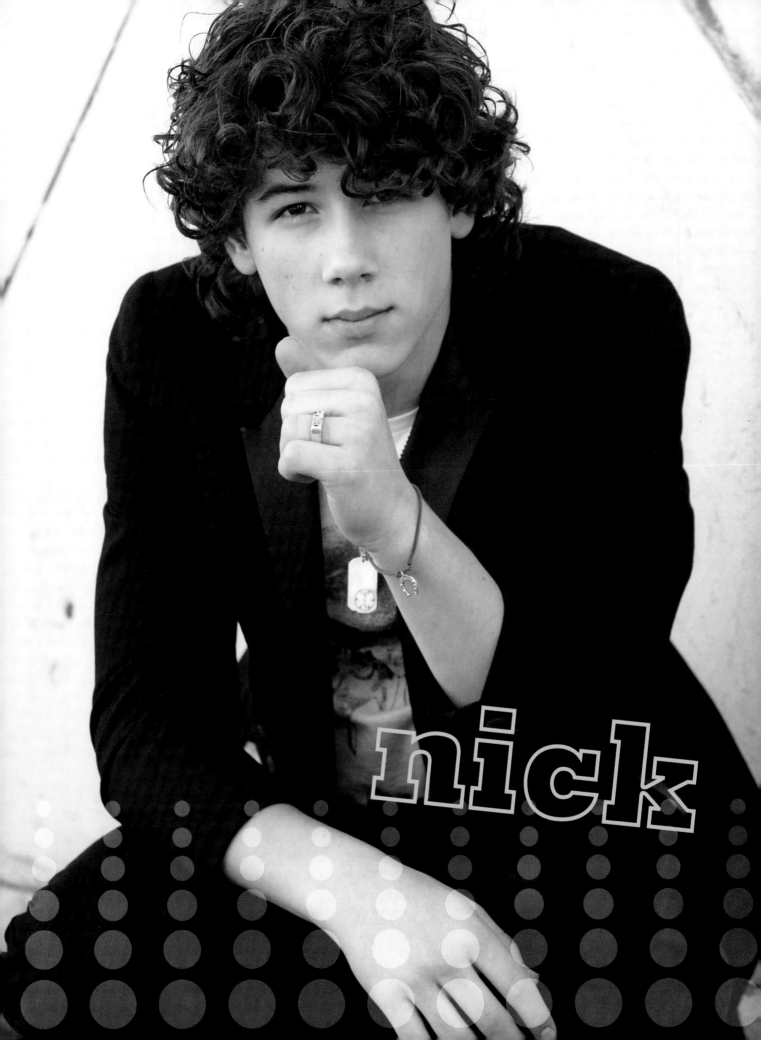

Kevin, Joe, and Nick's Best Celeb Pals!

The Jonas Brothers are extremely loyal to their friends. Kevin once drove Nick way out of his way—all to visit a friend! "I got stuck in eight hours of traffic!" Kevin remembered to *Tiger Beat* in June 2008. "That was really nice of him," Nick said, patting his big bro on the back. It was also really nice of Nick to make the journey to visit a friend in the first place—but that's just the way they roll!

As for stars, "We have a few celebrity friends on our Sidekick phones," Kevin told *Bop* in March 2007. "JoJo, Aly and AJ—they're awesome. Ricky Ullman, Jess from the Veronicas. We toured with them. We met JoJo through the Michalka sisters."

A list of their *closest* celebrity friends would include:

DEMI LOVATO

Of all their female friends, fellow rocker Demi Lovato is the closest. They all first met during auditions—but they weren't auditions for *Camp Rock*!

"Demi's awesome—she's a fantastic actress and a great singer! She's become like a little sister," Kevin told *Popstar!* in July 2008. "We actually first met her in the audition for *JONAS*. We read with her. She read with us. She ended up not getting the role there." But then, when tryouts came around for *Camp Rock*, Demi and Joe displayed dazzling chemistry in their screen tests together.

Working together on *Camp Rock* sealed the deal. Demi Lovato told *Bop* in August 2008, "When the Jonas Brothers first got to the set of the movie, I was kind of intimidated. I was, like, 'Whoa, they are for real.'" But she warmed up to the down-to-earth guys, and claimed she never crushed on any of them, not even Joe. "He felt more like a brother to me. The Jonas Brothers rock out. And they are so talented. They are a total inspiration."

"I was surprised by how down-to-earth they are!" Demi told *Twist* in its May/June 2008 issue. "They're people I'm going to stay in touch with."

Since then, they've bonded over shared goals—and they now even share the same management team. In fact, the guys wrote songs for Demi's debut CD, *Don't Forget*, and invited her to tour with them on the Burning Up Tour in the summer of 2008.

Nick's advice for Demi in *Tiger Beat* in August 2008 was, "Have fun and take a little time before each show to clear your head. Demi has a good head on her shoulders. I think she'll do all right."

ASHLEY TISDALE AND VANESSA HUDGENS

High School Musical starlet Ashley got to know the brothers when they moved into a house down the street from her in Los Angeles. Kevin told *Popstar!* in November 2007, "It's so weird because within a three-block radius, there's us, Miley, Vanessa, Zac, Corbin, and Ashley . . . everyone!"

"Ashley Tisdale came over when we had a pool party!" Joe told *Popstar!* in November 2007. "Yeah, she drove her Porsche over to our house. She won't let me drive it yet," Kevin added.

Ashley is a great neighbor and loyal friend—she's also attended several of their concerts over the years.

"We love Ashley," Joe said of the *High School Musical* star. "And [fellow *High School Musical* star] Vanessa's a lot of fun to hang around with. We have a great time!" Nick called them both sweet, and Kevin gushed, "Ashley's so amazing and beautiful! She's a really good friend of mine. And Vanessa is really funny. I have a good time with her."

HONOR SOCIETY

Some fans associate the rising band Push Play with the Jonas Brothers, but the connection is mainly through Mandy Van Duyne, who has dated both Joe Jonas and Push Play's CJ Baran and who is a big supporter of both groups. The Jonas Brothers have a much deeper connection with Honor Society, a fellow New Jersey band that features Alex Noyes, the former drummer from their backing band.

Alex told *Popstar!* in August 2008 he met Kevin Jonas when they attended high school together, then lost contact when Alex went off to college for a year. "He called me over the summer and was like, 'Listen, I got this opportunity; my brothers are in a band." Alex became the JoBros' first drummer. "There are a lot of great memories," he said. "I think our second show we ever did . . . was at the PNC Bank Arts Center opening up for the Backstreet Boys. I remember we'd only been a band for a month. The biggest venue I had ever played was about one hundred people, just with local bands, and you just walk out there on stage just like it's going to be a normal show and you just look and you're like, 'That's a lot of people!'"

Alex eventually left, forming Honor Society with Michael Bruno, Jason Rosen, and Andrew Lee, and the JoBros have been supportive of them ever since. In a show of solidarity, the guys attended Honor Society's August 5, 2008, gig at the

Knitting Factory in New York City, watching from the balcony.

In November 2008, Honor Society were lucky enough to open for the Jonases in special concerts in San Diego, Las Vegas, and Hollywood. Hey, that's what friends are for, right? But the Jonas Brothers have also forged a business relationship with Honor Society, signing them to a production deal and committing to launch them as the next big thing.

ROONEY

Touring together has made the Jonas Brothers fast friends with Rooney. Taylor Locke from the band has said that the Jonas Brothers are "nice guys and they've treated us well." When asked how they felt to be asked to tour with JB, lead singer Robert Carmine told *Tiger Beat Celebrity Spectacular!* in Summer 2008, "We were very excited. We didn't have any plans to go on the road and it was fun to know there was a tour in a week to go tour in arenas. It was pretty exciting. We had met them before and they were fans of our band."

RUMOR PATROL: TOP JONAS RUMORS DEBUNKED!

#7 The JoBros Don't Play Their Instruments!

Some anti-fans believe that the Jonas Brothers don't really play their own instruments. This was addressed in *Tiger Beat Celebrity Spectacular!* in Summer 2008 when Kevin said, "We perform our songs and play all of the instruments. I taught myself how to play guitar."

#6 Joe's Dating Demi Lovato and/or Selena Gomez!

In "The m Insider" for March 2008, the teen mag's deputy editor insisted that there were rumors floating around linking Joe to both Demi and Selena, but then went on to dash the rumors, stating, "Selena would never date a guy her friend may secretly like!"

#5 Zac Efron Stole Joe's Hair!

In May 2007 *Bop* dispelled the rumor that Zac Efron copied Joe's hairstyle, pointing out that Zac's shorter, spikier, darker locks were for his role in *Hairspray*, and were in no way inspired by Joe's faux-hawk.

#4 Kevin's in the Hospital!

In late 2007, rumors circulated that Kevin had been hospitalized. "I'm not sick at all," he told *Tiger Beat* in its January/February 2008 issue. "It was the weirdest rumor."

#3 Kevin Got Married!

Kevin told *Twist* in its May/June 2007 issue that the stupidest Jonas rumor he'd ever heard was "that I got married. Which is not true!" The rumor probably started thanks to the ring—a purity ring—that he always wears.

#2 Joe's Dating Miley!

In December 2007 *Twist* printed a rumor that Joe—not Nick—was dating Miley Cyrus! "That rumor is definitely not true!" Miley's publicist told the magazine, and history proved she wasn't lying!

#1 Nick's Being Paid Not to Smile!

Fan-generated rumors that Nick was being paid *not* to smile by his record company, Hollywood, came about when he suddenly seemed uniformly serious in all of his publicity photos. Nick told *Twist* in April 2008, "Next to my brothers, I'm the serious one, for sure." But this rumor was denied. "Nick's just very focused," Joe added.

the Jonas Brothers in and on love!

Though their music is #1 for them, the Jonas Brothers are just like other boys their age—easily distracted by girls! Just because they've told all the teen magazines they're "too busy to date anyone," that doesn't mean they're not secretly crushing on girls or even having private relationships far from the prying eyes of the press and their own protective fans.

"None of us believe in dating lots of people—we want to find that special person and to be with that person," Kevin told *Life Story*. But even so, the Jonas Brothers have been linked to several famous and not-so-famous girls, and they've got lots of opinions on the subject of dating.

It's no surprise that the boys treat girls they're interested in with respect. "Our dad says to just take your time with girls, walk with integrity and be respectful," Kevin said in *m* in July 2008.

Denise Jonas expects potential Jonas girlfriends to return the favor. "I want them all to find girls who respect them, girls who are not all about themselves," Denise Jonas told *J-14* in its May/June 2007 issue. "There are times that there are other priorities, so they have to be flexible. My sons are great guys—they would be great boyfriends for any girl."

You can see why their mom is their favorite girl! "Our hearts always seem to get broken on Valentine's Day," Joe told *m* in March 2007. "But no matter what our GF situation is, we always feel special on V-day—because of our mom. Every Valentine's Day, we wake up to a box of our favorite candy and a note that she's left for us on the dining room table."

Keep reading to find out everything you need to know about each of the Jonas brothers when it comes to girls . . . and see if you have a chance with any of them!

NICK JONAS: THE KEY TO HIS HEART

OLD-SCHOOL ROMEO!

Nick is an old-fashioned kind of guy who believes boys should ask girls out, not the other way around. "I like a girl who acts like a lady," Nick told *Bop* in April 2008. "I'll be the gentleman and she'll be the lady."

This attitude matches the values instilled in them by their parents. "We really feel that it is important to be a gentleman—that's how we were raised," Nick insisted to *J-14* in December 2007. "I find that girls really like it when you are like that. I'll open a door for a girl, and she'll be like, 'Oh, no one's done that for me in a really long time.'" Kevin agreed, saying, "I think guys should still open a door for a girl every chance they get, every time. They should try to take care of a girl as much as possible. She's like a princess, no matter what."

At the end of the day, Nick is a true romantic. "I know that true love is definitely out there," Nick told *J-14* in April 2008.

WHAT KINDS OF GIRLS HE LIKES!

Back in 2006, a fourteen-year-old Nick told *Bop*, "I would have to say that eyes are the first thing I look at. If they have beautiful eyes, I'm definitely interested!"

"I don't really have a type," Nick told *Bop* in September 2008. "Personality is a really big thing with me. Be interesting to talk to. That's important to me." His stance is further clarified by a quick perusal of *Tiger Beat*'s January/February 2008 issue. "I think when you create a specific type, it kind of messes with everything. If you only date one kind of person, you could miss a really good opportunity."

Still, even if he won't narrow it down to blondes, brunettes, or redheads, there are certain qualities he looks for.

"I want an intellectual girl who I can have a nice conversation with," Nick told *J-14* in September 2008, "because we'll talk more on the phone than in person. Looks don't really matter as long as the heart is right."

"I think for me, what I look for in a girl is that she's got to have a good personality—energetic, because I'm *not* that energetic," Nick told *Fans' Choice: Jonas Brothers—Living the Dream!*

He likes fun-loving girls who will be able to understand his insane schedule. "I want a GF who likes to have fun and just chill, even if it's for, like 20 minutes," Nick

> If all three of the JoBros likes a girl, they give each other a secret gesture, Joe told *Popstar!* in July 2007. "We snap our fingers. We would do that to each other and when she's not looking, we'd give each other the *look*." So what's the look? A head tilt/eyebrow wiggle combo!

told m in July 2008. "We're very busy, so just to be able to say 'Hi' and 'What's up?' on the phone and still have a great time is cool."

Nick is a sensitive guy who is in touch with his emotions—he's not afraid to open up, and you shouldn't be afraid to let him. "Listening and caring about what your crush says are good things," Nick advised in *Bop* in April 2007. "Talking on the phone is a good way to know your crush. Don't be afraid to talk to your parents about your crush."

"You should be able to share everything with your girlfriend," Nick told *J-14* in January 2008. If you feel you're a good listener, you and Nick might be a match made in heaven.

WHAT *NOT* TO DO!

"It's too *hard* having girlfriends," Nick told *Twist* in April 2007. What exactly is so hard about having a girlfriend? He's got plenty of reasons.

One of the biggest no-nos for Nick is if a girl is just into him because he is a star. In *Tiger Beat* in 2008, Nick admitted, "I'm probably the most reserved and conservative when it comes to dating. Everybody has a time when they need somebody to be there for them." He went on to say, "You have to kind of test them to see if they'd be your friend if you weren't in a band. There have been tons of cases where a girl was really nice—almost too nice—and I started to think, 'Would she be that nice if I weren't in a band?'"

Another thing to avoid if you wanna get with Nick is doing anything just to impress him. Some girls are shy about silly things when they're with boys, always worrying about what he'll think. For example, "It's so annoying when a girl is afraid to eat in front of you," Nick told *Twist*'s September 2006 issue. Isn't that a relief? You can go on a date with Nick and eat to your heart's content.

"Guys like it when girls aren't afraid to eat in front of them," Nick told *Tiger Beat* in March 2007. "My thing is steak with sweet potato, spinach, some bread sticks. And she has to let me pay. I always have to pay. It's the gentlemanly thing to do!"

Nick picks up on disrespectful behavior since he is himself so considerate. "I don't understand why girls talk to their friends while we're on the phone. It's like, 'Uhhh, talk to me!'" Nick told *Twist* in February 2008.

He's also against being wishy-washy.

Nick told *J-14* in January 2008, "The thing I hate more than anything is when . . . someone says, 'The ball is in your court!' That is the worst thing in the world for me! That is so annoying—when you're in a relationship, there are two people. It should be 50/50."

One big problem with dating Nick is his schedule. This is unavoidable! But he has some advice for potential GFs. "Encourage instead of discourage," Nick said in *Tiger Beat*'s January/February 2008 issue. "Instead of getting mad that I'm always gone, be happy when I can be there. That's cool and it's a good time."

But the most important thing to remember about Nick and his brothers is

DID YOU KNOW?

In *Teen* in Summer 2008, in one of Nick's handwritten answers to a questionnaire, he admitted he thinks that Demi Lovato is "really cute!"

that they are chill— they do not tolerate needless drama.

Nick even said to *Twist* in February 2007, "If a girl talks about drama at school or her past boyfriend or anything like that, then she's history."

HOW YOU CAN TELL IF NICK LIKES YOU!

One of the first signs that Nick is feeling a girl is if he begins to dole out the praise. "I used to rush into things a lot," Nick said to *Popstar!* in July 2007. "Then I realized that doesn't work too well. So I started taking the time to get to know the girl and stuff. I find that better to do. But if it's really awesome right away, I'll jump into it! I'm the kind of guy that'll give compliments. That's my thing."

Otherwise, Nick is superhard to read. "I still get shy talking to girls!" Nick told *Twist* in September 2008. This shyness leads to conflicting behaviors.

For example, Nick admitted to *Bop* in December 2007 that he has *avoided* girls he likes. "If I like a girl, there's a chance I don't know what she's thinking. So I start to question the situation. I want her to notice me, so I play it cool."

"I have a tendency to sort of look away when I start to like a girl," Nick confessed to *Twist* in March 2008. "So if I have to work hard to look in her eyes and be engaging during a conversation, then I know it's cool and it's for real."

Maybe one reason for his inability to hold eye contact is that he places so much importance in a girl's eyes as being windows to her soul. Nick told *Bop* in February 2008 he kinda-sorta believes in love at first sight. "It depends, but when you get to know somebody and you look in their eyes, and if there's a connection, it's like, 'Hey, I know that person!'"

But just as likely as he is to avoid a girl he likes, Nick sometimes does just the opposite.

"A major sign I'm falling for someone is when I want to hang out with her all the time," Nick told *Bop* in January 2008. "I want to talk to her and really get to know her."

One final thing to watch out for is if Nick gives you special gifts, especially anything related to music. "I wrote out a song in my handwriting for a girl," Nick revealed to *J-14* in February 2008. "It was pretty sweet—nice and old-looking. I burnt the edges of the paper. It was pretty cool!"

Basically, the real way to know if Nick likes you is to trust your instincts. If you have any question in your mind that he might like you, he probably does—and it'll just be a matter of time before he finds the right way to express it.

DATING NICK JONAS!

Nick and his brothers are very social— they've gone on lots of dates. You might be surprised to learn that most of their dates are not glamorous.

"I usually just hang out at Starbucks or Pinkberry," Nick told *Twist* in March 2008.

Nick has said he thinks the best dates happen in random places, but his all-time best date happened in the most obvious setting. "My best date was in a movie theater, and it was a group thing. We were seeing *Pirates of the Caribbean* and all these people were there and they were taking pictures. So it was really awkward. It was cool, though!" Nick told *Twist* in its May/June 2008 issue.

Even though dating disasters happen to the best of us, Nick has said he's been lucky enough to avoid them. Nick told *J-14* in January 2008, "I've never had the first-kiss, bumping-heads thing like that ever. Over this past year, I have seen a lot more [ups and downs in relationships] than I have in the past. Not so much heartbreak. I've never really gotten my heart broken yet—so I'm doing good." (Sadly, this would have been prior to his high-profile split with Miley Cyrus!)

Nick actually has the ideal spot picked out for an important date—if he ever asks you out and you end up there, that will be proof Nick thinks the world of you!

"Once, Kevin, Joe and I were staying at a Four Season hotel. There was an outside garden area and I was like, 'This would be a fun spot to hang out with a girl!' There was a huge heat blower, so you'd throw something at it and it would shoot up in the air," Nick told *Twist* in April 2008.

But if you don't want to wait until he makes a move, you could surprise him with a date he'll never forget—and I can tell you exactly what he's hoping for!

"My dream date would be for a girl to take me to a Yankees baseball game," Nick told *Bop* in August 2007. "She would win so many points if she did that!"

GIRLFIGHT!

Think the guys have enough girls after them that they never need to fight? Guess again! Nick spilled to *Twist* in July 2008, "There'll be a girl that I'm freaking out about. And she'll have an 'I love Kevin' shirt on! It's never a serious fight, but it's funny 'cause I'll think, 'Dude, she's into me!' and then she ends up being in love with Joe or Kevin."

In the same issue, Joe confirmed this dilemma. "Sometimes I see a very pretty girl in the audience and I think, 'I hope she's a fan of me,' and then I realize that she's Nick's fan—because she's holding a sign that says, 'Nick, look at me,' or 'Nick, I'm your wife and you just don't know it.' And I'm like, 'Oh, bummer.'"

NICK'S INSECURE, TOO!

"I'm insecure about my breath," Nick admitted to *m* in its October/November 2008 issue. "I'm always putting mints in my mouth so it smells good."

127

NICK'S GUIDE TO FLIRTING!

Sure, Joe is the #1 flirt of the brothers, but Nick knows a thing or two about the subject. "Technically, flirting is a dangerous thing because you never know if someone is flirting with you or just giving you a compliment. There is an actual difference."

"You need to be careful not to read too much into anything because things can easily be misinterpreted," Nick cautioned in *J-14* in February 2008. "Someone might say, 'Oh, you look really pretty today.' If I said that to you in person, you would be like, 'Oh, thanks,' but if you text-messaged that to some people, they would take that in a different way."

This goes both ways. "Boys don't really know what they're doing half the time," Nick told the same magazine in April 2008. "Sometimes I'm oblivious to flirting, and I just have to ask, 'Okay, what's the deal? Are you into me or not?' Or I'm the last one to even realize that I *have* a girlfriend until someone mentions it."

One way he tests a girl's intentions is in how she hugs. Nick told *Bop* in May 2008, "There's a rule someone taught me. If it lasts three seconds, she's trying to say, 'I'm just, like, whatever.' If it's five seconds, it's, 'I like you, you're cool.' If it's more than 10 seconds, then it's all good!"

And finally, don't forget that flirting can lead to disaster if it's done between BFFs. Nick believes guys and girls *can* be "just friends." But it's not easy! "It's possible," he told *Bop* in May 2008. "It just comes down to trying your hardest not to be flirtatious in any way. You don't want to be leading them on."

NILEY: THE TRUTH ABOUT NICK JONAS & MILEY CYRUS

"I know I've been in love," Nick told *J-14* in February 2008. "But I waited a long time before I used the word 'love' to a girl other than my mom. Love to me is more than just a word."

Who has Nick Jonas been in love with? Undoubtedly, Miley Cyrus would fit that bill. The two dated for almost two years in what became one of Hollywood's worst-kept secrets.

The first their fans knew of any possible romance was when Nick was spotted hanging out with Miley Cyrus at her *Total Request Live* appearance in June 2006. This rumor did not go over well— Nick was just becoming a heartthrob, and it never pleases fans to see the boy of their dreams "taken" so soon. But with no confirmation, the rumor remained just that— a rumor.

"I just think it's funny," Nick told *J-14*, seeming to deny he and Miley were more than pals. "Because you take a picture with somebody, then automatically you're dating. I just laugh it off."

Upping the ante, Nick admitted to having a crush on Miley Cyrus in the October/November 2006 issue of *Twist*, saying, "She's pretty cute." In the same issue, he mentioned that he'd met a very special girl through Zac Efron, a girl who he had thought would intimidate him before they met.

"I was really excited to meet this girl. Zac Efron hooked it up. At first, I thought I'd be at a loss for words, but then we connected." Hmmm! Note that Nick and Miley first met at an Elizabeth Glaser Pediatric AIDS event . . . and Zac Efron was at that event with his own then-secret GF, Vanessa Hudgens. Just saying!

Nick later seemed to confirm this theory himself in an interview with *Twist*. "I met [Miley] June 11, 2006. We were at a pediatric AIDS event. I had a big, total crush on her. We talked for a while and it was cool." He even told the magazine to listen for a couple of songs on *Jonas Brothers*, implying they could be about Miley. But according to this interview, Nick and Miley dated briefly in the summer of 2006 before parting ways. "It was a summer thing. We're just friends now and it's all good!" Still, it seems obvious Nick was fibbing and that the couple had never broken up at all.

Just when the rumor of the couple—dubbed "Niley" by fans—was dying down, Nick raised eyebrows again by admitting in the May 2007 issue of *Bop*, in a handwritten survey, that Miley Cyrus was his celebrity crush!

In its May/June 2007 issue, *Twist* announced that 60 percent of its readers voted they'd like to see Miley and Nick dating, representing a slight uptick in their approval. Little did fans know, the two were *already* an item!

"I am *not* going out with Nick," Miley claimed to *m* in May 2007. "I love him to death, and, of course, he's so hot! But we are too close of friends for anything to happen. It would just be way too weird! One thing's for sure, any girl who does end up with him is really lucky! He's adorable

As part of Disney's big push for the JoBros, the guys were signed up to appear in a special episode of *Hannah Montana*.

"It doesn't feel real," Kevin told *Bop* in October 2007. Joe agreed, saying, "It's cool that we weren't written in as characters. We don't have to really act—we are just ourselves." Nick said, "We still get excited about every little thing that happens to us, let alone something as major as appearing on the #1 tween series."

On the set of the episode, which was titled

These pictures show the Jonas Brothers and Miley Cyrus on the exact day they met, at an Elizabeth Glaser Pediatric AIDS Foundation event in June 2006!

"Me and Mr. Jonas and Mr. Jonas and Mr. Jonas," the guys were seen nervously studying their lines in between takes. To cut the tension, they would burst into song, wowing the cast. There was even a report of Kevin playfully coaching series costar Emily Osment on how to act out a hug by hugging her over and over!

During filming, there was a lot of goofing around. Kevin used an air-pump gun to shoot spongeballs at the rigging and overhead lights, clumsy Joe knocked down two mic stands while filming a scene with Billy Ray Cyrus, and Kevin accidentally whacked Nick on the head a little harder than the scene called for!

But the episode was completed, and it aired August 17, 2007, right after the premiere of *High School Musical 2* on Disney Channel. "Me and Mr. Jonas and Mr. Jonas and Mr. Jonas" was the highest-rated episode of *Hannah Montana* ever, with over 10.7 million viewers—a pretty good TV debut for the three-pack of new thespians!

and sweet—just a really great guy."

"I am not dating Miley Cyrus," Nick told *Popstar!* in July 2007. "I mean yeah, she's pretty, but I didn't date her."

Yet, behind the scenes, Niley was real. The couple spent time together whenever possible and their families became intertwined. The pair did normal things that any couple would do, and cherished the times when they were not being watched.

"When we're at home in California," Nick told *Twist*, "we like to ride bikes around the neighborhood or get Pinkberry. It's usually Miley, me, and my brothers just hanging out. We've had one of those

things where it's always just kind of there."

After being discreet for so long, the pair began to slip up. Miley told Ellen DeGeneres that Nick was her favorite Jonas Brother and told *Twist* in February 2008, "I went to Nick's house once and left a card on his door that said, 'Take two steps forward. Take two steps to the side. Turn around 10 times.' And when he turned around, I was there!" Clearly, this is something you do with a boyfriend, not a friend.

Also changing was JoBros' fans acceptance. At least some of the guys' fans felt Miley was some kind of bad influence, while others were just upset that Nick might not be single. In late 2007, Nick began denying he was dating "Hannah Montana," which fans took to mean he was deliberately not saying "Miley Cyrus" in order to avoid outright lying. *Popstar!* asked him to clarify in January 2008, and he offered, "Oh, no, I just say that 'cause most people know her as that as well, so if they don't know her as Miley, I just say Hannah Montana."

Meanwhile, Miley continued to imply publicly that she and Nick might be more than friends. "He hates me because I always text him and I'm like, 'Whatcha doin'? Come see me, I'm bored!'" she told *Bop* in October 2007.

Then came news that the Jonas Brothers would be joining Miley on her Best of Both Worlds Tour in the last part of 2007, affording the couple tons of together time that made some fans extremely jealous. Negative comments about Miley on fan sites became the norm.

In *Twist* in December 2007, Miley said, "I'm really excited to be on tour with Nick. He's like my best friend. Yesterday, I got up and went to see him at 7:30 in the morning just because I really wanted to see him! Whether we're together or not, no matter what, we're really close friends and that's what I love." Nick said, "I'm really excited! We were really busy when we were away from each other last summer."

Of Miley, Nick told *J-14* in January 2008 that there could be something between them. "I think there is . . . maybe," he said. He also said that touring with Miley would be helpful because "in the past, we haven't been touring together, so there's been distance. It gets kind of hard."

When Miley and the Jonas Brothers were touring together, the normally high-energy diva began feeling run down. "I kept getting really sick," she told *m* in its October/November 2008 issue. "One night, Nick stopped by my room and I wasn't feeling great. He suggested that I test my blood sugar like he does, since he's diabetic. I did, and my blood sugar was really low—it was bad!" This led to a professional diagnosis of hypoglycemia. Miley credited Nick with "saving her life" for his advice.

Miley was supportive of Nick's private struggle with diabetes. "'Nick, are you sure you're okay?'" he quoted her as asking him, in *Twist* in July 2007. "She was there to support me. It felt good."

Nick also counseled Miley when a mutual friend died at thirteen years old from cystic fibrosis while they were on the Best of Both Worlds Tour. Clearly, these two went through a lot together.

As a symbol of their mutual affection, Nick and Miley wore matching dog tags in late 2007. Nick also bought Miley a bracelet from Tiffany's for her fifteenth birthday, and Miley admitted to *Bop* in February 2008 that she had bought Nick a polo that said "Best Friends Forever."

"All the Jonas Brothers will be with me on tour," Miley told *Twist* in January 2008. "So we're having our Christmas party at the Trump Hotel. We're going to hang out in a little ballroom type thing and make it Christmassy." She went on to say she was hoping for roses, jewelry, or something homemade from Nick.

"I've never had a girlfriend during Christmastime. But I think the perfect holiday scenario would be Christmas in New York City. I'd like to go down to Central Park, hang out by the ice skating rink, possibly Rockefeller Center. There's a couple things you've just gotta see when you're in New York City," Nick told *Twist* in January 2008. "Sadly, I haven't had a New Year's kiss yet, but hopefully I will this year."

By the time the two were appearing on *Dick Clark's New Year's Rockin' Eve*, the press had picked up rumors of a shocking breakup. Soon, the couple would only pose in pictures together if they were not directly side by side.

BEAUTIFUL MUSIC TOGETHER!

Did you know Nick and Miley almost wrote a song together? In *Bop* in February 2008, Miley confessed, "Nick and I thought about writing a song and singing it together. That'd be so cool."

"She's a heartbreaker, that's for sure," Nick joked to *Life Story* in Winter 2008, but was he kidding? Rumor had it that Miley's heart had been stolen by V Factory member Wesley Quinn. But when checking out of the Trump Hotel—the very place where Nick and Miley had just shared a fab holiday party and then a not-so-fab breakup—Nick refused to believe it. "I don't like to comment about that sort of thing!" he told *Twist* in March 2008. "I'll leave that up to those 'sources'!"

Mitchel Musso spilled the beans to *Popstar!* in April 2008 on the demise of Niley, saying, "She called me and was like, 'We're not together.' Miley talks to me about relationships. Their tour was over, so now she doesn't see him every day. It must be hard, you know? He is probably around girls all the time, and she's around guys all the time." Mitchel went on to say Miley used to fume when Nick didn't call her back, and that overall their split was "a timing thing" and that there was no cheating because "they're both really cool people. I never got from her, like, that there was something wrong."

"He never wanted to talk about Miley," said Rooney's Taylor Locke in *Twist*'s May/June 2008 issue after the band had toured with the boys. "At first, I didn't even know they'd broken up. But, he *was* writing songs all the time."

"It seemed really quick," Cody Linley told *J-14* in its May/June 2008 issue. "I was really surprised. The last I heard, they loved each other. We talked about her and Nick before on the set, and he'd call and she'd be so lovey-dovey with him, like she wanted to marry him! I was pretty shocked when I heard the news."

"There is a lot of stuff that went on, but Miley is totally fine," Aly Michalka spilled to *m* in April 2008. "She's strong-willed." She went on to describe her and her sister AJ's advice to Miley. "We said, 'Look, you deserve better. You need to be with a guy that treats you right.'"

For his part, Nick said to *J-14*, "Miley is a great friend. We love her, you know? We had a great time on tour with her. I think for us, we just try to stay focused and do what we've been doing."

"She's our friend and we'll always have her back," he reiterated to *Rolling Stone*.

The guys' first-ever *Rolling Stone* cover story was noteworthy for two reasons. For one thing, it contained some quotes from Nick about Miley that seemed to confirm that they had dated, and that they were no longer together.

"There was a point in our lives when we were very close," Nick told *Rolling Stone* of Miley. "We were neighbors when we were on tour together. It was good. Just really close."

For another, it spelled out a new rumor—that Nick was dating Selena Gomez, a new Disney Channel star whom Miley and her BFF Mandy Jiroux had mocked in a widely seen YouTube video.

Then, the other shoe dropped when Miley gave an eye-opening interview to

Seventeen in September 2008, completely spilling her guts on their romance.

"We became boyfriend and girlfriend the day we met," Miley said, breaking the silence. "He was on a quest to meet me, and he was like, 'I think you're beautiful and I really like you.' And I was like, 'Oh, my gosh, I like *you* so much.' Nick and I loved each other. We *still* do, but we were *in love* with each other. For two years, he was basically my 24/7. But it was really hard keeping it from people. We were arguing a lot, and it really wasn't fun." Miley went on to reveal that they argued about their schedules. "But when we were actually *together*, it was great." The breakup came just before they went onstage. "Is this just too much for us right now?" Miley asked Nick, who agreed. "We were both crying on that last day we were together."

Miley went on to tell *Seventeen* that Nick wanted her to get highlights in her hair, implying he had domineering opinions of how she should look. After they parted ways, she went Goth. "I was rebelling against everything Nick wanted me to be." She also called their relationship "a little too cliché for me," likening it to Brad and Angelina's high-profile partnership. The response to this breach of privacy? Well, Kevin was seen wearing a "Team Demi & Selena" T-shirt that week while on his way to one of the band's Madison Square Garden shows. Ouch! The message could not have been more clear—back off, Miley!

The ultimate final chapter might have been when Miley released the single "7 Things," about an ex-boyfriend she hates. Fans were shocked—she could only be talking about Nick, right?

"Nick is someone that was really important in my life but I don't hate him," Miley told *Popstar!* in November 2008. When asked if he thought the song might be about him, Nick told the same magazine, "I think it's funny. Honestly, I'm not insecure, my friends are cool—so it can't be about me! At the end of the day, I just laugh at it."

Sadly, Niley was not only over, it had ended somewhat badly!

NELENA: HAS NICK FOUND TRUE LOVE WITH SELENA GOMEZ?

On or off the record, Nick and Selena have been dating since early 2008, around the time he and Miley broke up.

Selena Gomez told *Twist* in February 2008, "I've heard a lot of rumors recently that Miley and I are fighting over Nick! It's not true, definitely not. I am not dating Nick, and we are all friends and just really get along. I always see Miley at events. She's so sweet! It's usually me and her or Emily hanging out and texting each other."

But despite this sunny version of events, Miley and her BFF Mandy Jiroux mercilessly mocked Selena and her BFF Demi Lovato in a YouTube video posted in March 2008. In the infamous video, the girls dressed up like exaggerated versions of Selena and Demi, made fun of their hair, makeup, and clothing, and even mocked Demi for having the gap between her front teeth fixed. Selena and Demi were shocked by this attack. Selena told *Popstar!* in July 2008, "Yeah, I don't really know what happened there . . . but I was surprised about it." Demi was at a loss for words, stammering, "Um . . . I don't . . . know. Like, I don't know! 'Cuz I don't know *them*. I was . . . *surprised*. I was kinda honored, but in the same way, um . . . *I don't know* . . . !"

It seemed obvious that Miley was jealous of Selena and was taking it out on her and Demi. The incident led to the video receiving over four million views, exploding into the mainstream press within a few months as a major entertainment story—despite the fact that the people involved in this high-profile love triangle were all just fifteen years old!

Selena, like Miley before her, was coy when discussing the dating rumors in *Popstar!* in July 2008. "Nick Jonas is *absolutely* amazing. He's one of the coolest people I've ever met and he's really passionate about what he does and that's what makes him awesome, I think. And he's got a great heart . . . but no, I'm not dating Nick."

Despite denials, further proof emerged when Selena and Nick were photographed separately wearing an identical vintage Elvis Costello shirt.

Of the matching shirts, Selena told *J-14* in its October/November 2008 issue, "It was pure coincidence. I got it at a vintage store, and I didn't know he had that shirt. It was a huge thing. I was like, 'Of course, this would happen to us.'" Selena told *Tiger Beat* in October 2008 that just because she and Nick were spotted wearing the same shirt, that didn't mean they were a couple. "I know that couldn't be more of a confirmation," she admitted, "but NO, we are not dating. Trust me, they are all great guys, but I don't see myself with him personally. I couldn't date a rock star because they are constantly on the road."

"It's hilarious. She's in our music video and she's come to a couple of shows because her best friend is Demi Lovato, and Demi is our opening act on the tour. We're just friends," Nick told *J-14* in the October/November 2008 issue.

But fans were skeptical.

Unbeknownst to most fans, Nick secretly attended Selena's Sweet 16 party, held July 20, 2008, at the Kress, a Hollywood hotspot. They made a deal that no photos would be taken, but Khloe Kardashian posed with Nick and her photos wound up on MySpace, proof that he was in the house for his GF's special day!

Once *Rolling Stone* published a picture showing Selena Gomez hugging Nick, fans' suspicions that the two were a couple came to a peak—fans began to accept that the two, dubbed "Nelena," were a true item.

"I'm hugging a friend, so obviously I'm dating," Nick said sarcastically to *J-14* in its October/November 2008 issue. "What's funny is that I was there and I hugged *all* the boys," Selena added.

But in *Twist*'s October/November 2008 issue, Nelena was confirmed in print—with undeniable evidence! In the September issue of the magazine, Selena had said, "I don't kiss on the first date," but related that her mystery crush had said, "I don't play by the rules." *Twist* noted that Nick had given the identical story to *GL*, also refusing to name his crush. The media had caught the secret couple red-handed!

"I've gotten extremely close with Nick and his family," Selena told the magazine. "That's what we are going to say right now." Nick said, "Selena's an amazing girl and any guy would be lucky to date her."

And that's where Nelena prefer to keep things—obvious, but not admitted. They seem devoted to the idea of keeping their private lives private.

nalyson: those alyson stoner rumors!

"There was flirting on set—we're teenagers! Nick's so sweet and sensitive and so cute. He'll give subtle hints, that's what I love!" Alyson Stoner said to *Twist* in January 2008 of Nick after meeting him while filming *Camp Rock*. Nick's response was to say, "Yeah, see, I didn't even know I did it, so I guess it is pretty subtle! But occasionally, you know, you've gotta drop hints. I'm not like Joe, though!"

But when asked in *m* in June 2008 if he'd ever dated any of his *Camp Rock* costars, Nick offered, "Alyson and I would hang out! Actually, Joe, Alyson, and I were constantly crashing parties—we even crashed a snack-food corporate party! We also had dance parties, which were really fun."

This answer led to rumors that he

and Alyson had been or were a couple. Alyson, having seen the grief Miley and Selena had gone through for daring to date the #1 teen heartthrob, was eager to set things straight.

"JUST FRIENDS!" she wrote in all caps on a handwritten diary entry for *Twist* when they asked her about Nick's cutest feature. "But he has a signature dance move that he'd use at the dance parties on set! It was pretty awesome!"

"I stay in touch with Nick, but I'm the last person who'd be in his dating circle! We have chemistry on-screen, but it's acting!" Alyson Stoner told *Twist* in its May/June 2008 issue.

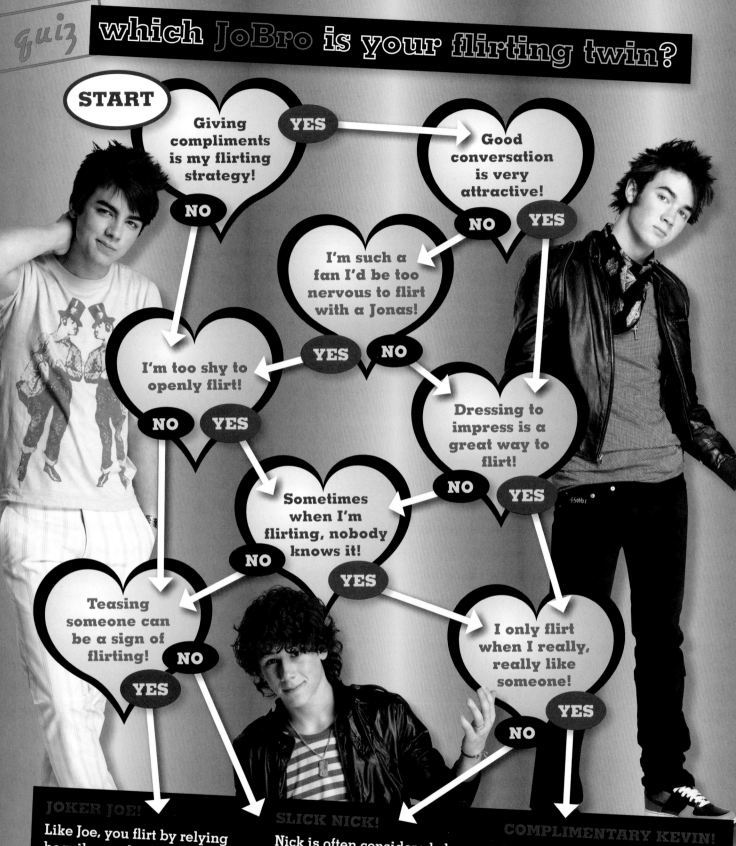

START

Giving compliments is my flirting strategy!

YES

Good conversation is very attractive!

NO

YES

NO

I'm such a fan I'd be too nervous to flirt with a Jonas!

YES

NO

I'm too shy to openly flirt!

NO

YES

Dressing to impress is a great way to flirt!

NO

YES

Sometimes when I'm flirting, nobody knows it!

NO

YES

I only flirt when I really, really like someone!

Teasing someone can be a sign of flirting!

NO

YES

NO

YES

NO

JOKER JOE!

Like Joe, you flirt by relying heavily on playful humor. Keeping things lighthearted means rejection is not such a big deal. You and Joe are also comfy going up to a person and saying "hi" the first time!

SLICK NICK!

Nick is often considered shy, but he's really more serious and introspective, just like you. When it comes to flirting, he tends to be smooth and under the radar. A simple smile is often the main strategy!

COMPLIMENTARY KEVIN!

Kevin loves to shower his crushes with compliments and conversation, an approach you've been known to take. It's not about clever pickup lines, it's about communication and sharing the moment!

JOE JONAS: THE GROUP'S BIGGEST LOVER BOY!

WHAT JOE LOOKS FOR IN A GIRL!

If you're curious what Joe's type is, I've got all the answers! First and foremost, as Joe told *Twist* in February 2007, "We like good girls. They can't smoke and we don't like drugs. Kevin, Nick, and I are in the no-drama zone."

Joe's desire to be with wholesome girls might be connected to how much he respects his mom, Denise. Joe told *Twist* in September 2008 that he was looking for love. "I'm looking for somebody who is really good to Mom!"

But along with strength of character, Joe wants a girl he can admire for her strength of personality.

"I like a girl who carries herself with confidence. And a girl who loves wearing dresses, dressing up even if she goes to the airport," Joe told *Life Story* in Winter 2008. No sloppy girls for Joe!

If you're the type of person who likes surprises and is physically active, Joe could be a great match for you. "I'm really adventurous, and one day I want to pack my suitcase and travel the world," Joe said to *m* July 2008. "So I'd like to meet somebody who'd do that with me." A good idea might be for you to write Joe an old-fashioned letter suggesting a journey, since he loves reading them! "I think it's cute when a girl writes me a letter—letters are always cool," Joe told *Bop* in April 2008. Lucky for him, he gets more fan mail every week than Elvis did back in the day!

CAMERA SHY!

The Jonas Brothers ban cameras when they're around girls they might be interested in—that means none of them are snapping photos, and the girls aren't allowed to, either. After all, the last thing they need is for a girl one of them is just beginning to get interested in posting gotcha photos on Flickr!

Joe also strongly admires girls who can sing or write songs. He told *Bop* in December 2006, "If she's talented, that's really cool. Every girl has something special about her. And it's cool if she can share it with everyone!" No wonder he's dated so many famous female faces!

137

HOW TO TURN JOE OFF!

"I think me, Kevin, and Nick are all about the no-drama zone. We don't like it when girls bring up drama too much—we don't want to hear about all your fights with your BFF. I wouldn't want to hear that, not on the first date at least," Joe told a fan in an advice column for *Twist* in February 2008.

And *not* talking about ex-boyfriends with your new boyfriend is pretty much a great piece of advice to follow with any guy, not just Joe.

In a more intimate admission, Joe opened up with *Life Story* in Winter 2008 to discuss something that truly bothers him in a potential GF. "I'm always disappointed when I'm into a girl and she brushes off something that's really important to me. When I'm excited about something, I want to share it with the people I love, and if the girl isn't excited for me, or at least excited that it's making me happy, well, that's a sign that something is wrong."

That certainly sounds like something that's happened to him in the past, doesn't it? Makes you wonder who hurt Joe's pride in this way.

Finally, Joe places a lot of stock in kissing! "Guys just want to kiss *you*, not your makeup, so too much lip gloss is not a good idea!" he advised in *m* in March 2008. You might be tempted to get all done up for Joe, but it turns out he prefers the natural look.

JOE'S IDEAL DATING GAME!

"About two weeks into it, if you're really into the person, you'll know if you want to go on a date," Joe told *J-14* in February 2008.

Joe's ideal NYC date would be ice-skating and a carriage ride through Central Park followed by a romantic dinner. "I know this very special place—it's a secret spot. It's upstairs in the Marriott Marquis Hotel in Times Square. There's this view that looks over Times Square, and there's this place where you can sit, and I always get a Shirley Temple."

"I want a girl to blindfold me and take me to Disneyland!" Joe told *Bop* in May 2008.

"I had a lot of fun getting sushi with Joe and a girl recently," Nick told *Twist* in August 2008. "We were really experimenting by eating all this crazy fish, so it was funny!"

All ideal dates end with a kiss, and Joe has definite ideas about how that part of the date should go, too! He told *m* in March 2008, "Kisses are perfect in front of a sunset. And I think it's better to be alone if it's your first kiss in a new relationship. Everyone else doesn't need to see it!"

FROM DORK TO SMOOTH OPERATOR!

Joe was not born an irresistible ladies' man. Hardly! When he was younger, he was actually . . . quite a dork!

"In kindergarten, I didn't know what to say to a girl I liked, so I blurted out, 'I like your red marker!' It was dumb," Joe recalled in *Twist* in March 2008.

Once, Joe had fallen for a local girl, but was too shy to approach her when he noticed her in an ice cream shop. So he came up with Plan B. "I had this Razor scooter that I thought was the coolest thing in the world," he told *J-14* in September 2008. "The first day of school, she was there, and I decided I would jump over the sidewalk right in front of her and she'd be like, 'Wow! Who's that guy?' I went flying by her, and I jumped on the side of the curb, but I got caught, flipped over and started rolling. She was like, 'Are you okay?' and I said, 'I'm fine! I'm fine!' and started to ride away. Ah, the scooter incident."

Being somewhat nerdy as a kid made Joe's transformation all the more exciting for him. Almost overnight, he picked up a guitar, found his inner rock star by performing, and went from being a dateless wonder to having girls screaming at his every move.

"When I was younger, there was this girl I liked. I guess it's different with every girl, but she would always, like, push her hair back, and I was like, 'Wow, I loved it,'" Joe told *J-14* in February 2008. He wasn't able to work up the nerve to ask that girl out, but now that he's a world-famous singer, Joe is making up for lost time, dating lots of girls without settling down into a serious relationship with any of them. After all, he's still young—nobody's in a rush to see him get married!

"A lot of girls are around now . . . I'm enjoying it," Joe told *CosmoGIRL!* in Summer 2008. He also joked to *Twist* in its May/June 2007 issue, "I heard that I was dating all of the swimsuit models in the world at the same time. No comment!"

"The most attractive thing about a girl is the little things," Joe told *Tiger Beat*'s January/February 2008 issue. "I think it's

always that one person who does something where you're like, 'Wow.'" Now, he's in a position where any girl who makes him think "wow" is a girl he could potentially date.

Of course, his fans are obsessed with knowing who, at any given moment, possesses Joe's heart.

"When I was young, I wanted to know what my favorite bands were up to all the time," he told *Rolling Stone*. "And it's funny when there's a rumor. It's funny when you find out there are other celebrities with crushes on you, like when I read that Lauren Conrad from *The Hills* liked me."

The former dork, who spent so much time crushing on unattainable girls, is in seventh heaven now that girls like Lauren Conrad are crushing on *him*!

WHEN JOE MAKES HIS MOVE!

Joe is the most flirtatious of the group. During an on-location photo shoot for *Twist* at an Ed Hardy store in 2006, Nick and Kevin posed in hats while Joe took off to try and make an impression on the salesgirl. "She's *wow*!" he told the magazine's writer.

"For me, it's about always trying to flirt with my crush," Joe admitted to *Bop* in January 2008. Unlike some boys, who complain about "games," Joe enjoys it when a girl confuses him about her true intentions at first—he likes the mystery.

Flirtatious Joe told *J-14* in February 2008, "Keep it playful for as long as you can—that's more fun. When you immediately tell your friend, 'Hey, tell him that I like him,' that kind of kills it. I like it when it's like, 'Let's just have fun with it for a while.'"

Making things challenging can sometimes be the best way to captivate Joe, especially since so many girls are throwing themselves at him right and left. "It's a lot of fun when I can't quite tell if someone likes me or not. It drives me crazy, and it's great, because the challenge means you can have an even longer relationship," Joe told *J-14*'s May/June 2008 issue. "Say there's another guy you think likes the girl—it can be a competition. Sometimes it's a good idea to make it hard for us boys!"

> "Joe likes to give hugs to certain people. He likes to pick them up and twirl them around and play with their hair."

According to *Tiger Beat* in its January/February 2008 issue, Joe keeps things light at first himself. He lets a girl know he likes her via "first-grade stuff" like nudging her and teasing her.

He's also the king of the cheesy pickup lines. "My favorite one is, 'You're like my library card 'cause I'm checkin' you out!'" Joe told *Twist* in April 2008.

But as Kevin told *J-14* in September 2008, Joe's flirting style *can* be direct— "He'll walk up to a girl on the street, out of nowhere, and say, 'Hey, how are you doing?' The girl will turn around to look . . . as if she's supposed to know who he is! It's really funny."

The direct approach is pretty easy for any girl to spot, even from a distance! "Joe likes to give hugs to certain people. He likes to pick them up and twirl them around and play with their hair," Joe's *Camp Rock* costar Alyson Stoner told *Twist* in January 2008.

Even though he's totally obvious, don't take that as an invitation to ask him on a date. Joe likes to be the one who asks a girl out, not vice versa. "I personally don't like it when girls do that!" he told *m* in June 2007. "I'd rather make the moves."

When Joe's ready to ask you out, he will not hesitate, especially if he senses there might be competition.

"It's better to take a risk than to wait around," Joe told *m* in March 2007. "You never know!"

"When I want to ask someone out, I get really excited," Joe told *J-14* in July 2007. "Of course, I get a little nervous beforehand, too, you know? But I get more excited than anything else around the girl because I just really want to ask her."

Joe is someone who truly relishes all aspects of dating, from first meeting the girl to a little cat-and-mouse flirting to asking her out and seeing how things will turn out. That little shy boy from New Jersey is having the time of his life!

BRO VS. BRO!

"There actually was one time when Kevin and I liked the same girl," Joe said in a rare admission to *Bop* in February 2007. "I was like, 'You know what, Kevin? If it doesn't work out between me and her, go for it.'" How generous of you Joe, lol!

More seriously, Joe truly does not get caught up in competition with his brothers for a girl.

"If you like the same girl as one of your best friends, you won't go after her, and we're best friends," Joe told *J-14* in September 2008 of their bro code. "I'd rather have my best friend than some girl we're fighting over."

JOE'S DATING DISASTERS!

He may be one of the cutest, most successful, and richest boys around, but not everything Joe touches turns to gold.

"There was this girl I liked, and she lived in a different country," Joe told *J-14* in December 2007. "I sent her a big bouquet of flowers, and sending flowers from a different country can be expensive . . ." Long-distance relationships are notoriously hard to maintain. With Joe Jonas, they have so far proved to be impossible. He told *J-14* in August 2008, "It's tough on tour because you're so far away from the person all the time. It's frustrating! After a while, you're like, 'Ugh! Where are you?'"

Joe loves dating so much that he absolutely dreads bad dates. He told *Twist* in March 2008, "If a first date's going badly and you're out to dinner at a nice place, you have to wait so long for your meal to come out! I'd rather just go to Bob's Big Boy. This way, if it's a bad situation, at least the food comes out really fast!"

Joe's worst date ever sounds like it would be one of the worst dates of all time for anyone!

"I went to the movies with a crush and we got followed by this creepy old lady. We kept leaving and going to a different movie because we were *that* freaked out, and she kept on following us! Plus, I was too embarrassed to have my mom come pick me up early!" Joe told *Twist* in its May/June 2008 issue.

Then there is Joe's bad timing—it's burned him more than once, especially around the holidays.

"I was going to surprise a girl I was seeing by sending flowers to her job. I wanted to throw her off, so even though I had already asked her to be my Valentine, I pretended something was wrong the day before. She was like, 'How are you doing?' and I said, 'Oh, fine, uh, I gotta go.' She wound up breaking up with me the night before Valentine's!" Joe told *Twist* in February 2008.

"I had a New Year's kiss once. But it was like, 'Let's start the year off together,' and then we wound up breaking up right after!" Joe told *Twist* in January 2008.

141

MANDY VAN DUYNE: JOE'S FIRST SERIOUS GF!

Blonde, beautiful Mandy Van Duyne first met the JoBros in 1996 at church. "Their dad was my pastor. I was close with all the boys, but Nicholas was my very best friend from Day One. We even had a spy club!" she remembered in *Fans' Choice: Jonas Brothers—Living the Dream!*

Mandy Van Duyne may have started out as a playmate of Nick's, but she eventually dated Joe Jonas for a time! "I used to hang out with her every day in New Jersey—we'd watch *S Club 7* on TV and sing songs," Nick said in the May/June 2006 issue of *Twist*. "I lost touch with her for a while when I did Broadway. Then I started hanging out with her again and she had really come out of her shell and [had] become a beautiful lady and [had] just become, you know, Mandy!"

This was when Joe pounced. The pair dated for months prior to Joe's rise to fame. Their romantic relationship ended, but their friendship has remained strong.

"Joseph and I had been best friends for years before we dated," Mandy said in *Fans' Choice: Jonas Brothers—Living the Dream!* "I have always loved him as a friend, so just because we broke up, those feelings we had as friends never go away. You have to get past the break-up and remember you were friends first and that is what is important!"

"Mandy is one of our best friends," Joe described to *Life Story*. "She grew up with us and I actually dated her, but then we broke up. But we're still best friends, which doesn't happen often. It didn't work out between us, but everything ended up okay."

Joe is a believer in trying to stay friends with girls after he breaks up with them—whenever possible. "When a guy and a girl break up, you should never lose that part of the friendship," he told *Twist* in January 2008.

In fact, Mandy herself met her longtime BF CJ Baran of Push Play at a Jonas Brothers press conference in July 2007! CJ, an admirer of the band, had shown up to promote Push Play and wound up one degree of separation from Joe by winning Mandy's heart.

AJ MICHALKA & JOE: TWEEN POWER COUPLE!

The Jonas Brothers became great pals of singers Aly & AJ Michalka after the groups toured together. They had so much in common—their music was aimed at the Radio Disney market, both of their families were devout Christians, both had family bands, and both believed in writing their own songs.

Asked by *Twist* in February 2006 about Aly & AJ, "Joseph" (as he was called professionally then) said, "We [Jonas Brothers] rock more because there are three of us and only two of them!" But he told *Twist* in the May/June 2006 issue simply, "They're our best friends!"

Secretly, Joe and AJ were more than friends—they began dating in early

2006 while on tour and kept it up for most of the year. The Jonas Brothers being tight with their fans from way back, many fans suspected Joe and AJ were hooking up, but both played dumb when asked about it.

For its August 2006 issue, *m* traveled to the Jonas family home in Wyckoff, where the boys spilled the beans about their tight bond with Aly & AJ. "Aly's always like, 'Nick, you're the adult, Kevin, you're serious, and Joe, you're just . . . forget you!'" Nick reported.

In the August 2006 issue of *m*, Joe said, "We're really close friends . . . They are cute girls. Maybe one day! But we're friends for now." Kevin chimed in, "We made a promise with Aly & AJ that we won't let this friendship die." Sadly, the girls and the Jonas Brothers are no longer close, thanks to what wound up being a bad breakup between Joe and AJ. Bringing an end to their liaison was AJ's decision to go public about her and Joe's relationship—without warning Joe first.

In *Twist* in January 2007, AJ was quoted confirming rumors that she and Joe Jonas were BF/GF! "It's true that we have been dating . . . life is good!" It warranted a mention on the magazine's cover and sent fans into a tizzy of "I told ya so!" vs. "Say it ain't so!" But by the following issue, the couple had split, sparking rumors that AJ's indiscretion about their pairing (she was sick of pretending) caused Joe discomfort.

"We both just went our separate ways," Joe told *J-14* in March 2007. "She's a really sweet girl and we're still friends. I don't want to talk about it, but, hey . . . I'm single!"

Giving more of a reason, Joe told *Popstar!* in July 2007, "It was a distance thing."

Since then, Aly & AJ and the Jonas Brothers have hardly spoken at all. Even though they share a record label, they don't even appear at events together.

AJ seems to be upset with Joe, but Joe isn't the jealous type—he later publicly shook hands with Ryan Sheckler, who everyone knew was dating AJ by then. "Other guys always ask me, 'How do you do that?' I'm just confident with myself," he told *Twist* in its May/June 2008 issue.

"Aly's always like, 'Nick, you're the adult, Kevin, you're serious, and Joe, you're just . . . forget you!'"

THE BATTLE FOR JOJO!

Joe told *Popstar!* in September 2006 that the guys' biggest fight ever—and their only one over a girl—was over JoJo.

"When we met JoJo, it was so funny! Nick was like, 'You know what? She likes me!' I'm like, 'Nick, give me a break! Come on, buddy! If she likes anybody, she's going to like *me*!' Then JoJo gave me her information just to hang out. And I'm like, 'Hey, Nick, you can have this . . . JoJo gave it to me.' He's like, 'Fine! Argh!'"

Comments like this led to rumors that Joe and JoJo were officially dating, which they denied.

But Nick (perhaps still smarting from losing out!) seemed to confirm the rumors by telling *m* in March 2007, in response to a question about competing for a crush, "It happened with me, Joe and JoJo! Joe was more serious about JoJo, until he found out she had a boyfriend." Joe even said, "As for me and JoJo in the future? My door's always open!"

In early 2008, the JoJo rumor swirled again when she was spotted with the guys and photographed arm in arm with Joe. "They stopped in my hometown on tour, so we all hung out," JoJo told *m* in April 2008. "I've known Joe for three years—we're just friends!"

"She had on superhigh heels, and I was helping her through the snow, as I would for my mom or any girl," Joe insisted to *CosmoGIRL!* in Summer 2008. "Somebody took pictures and suddenly we became JoeJo. I just laughed because it was ridiculous."

If you're not sure whether to believe Joe and JoJo, both of whom have good reason for not wanting fans to flip out, you have to admit that Denise Jonas would never lie! Mama J told *Twist* in March 2008, "They're *not* dating," and the legend of "JoeJo" evaporated almost as soon as it had appeared!

DEMI LOVATO: JOE'S GIRL FRIEND OR JOE'S GIRLFRIEND?

Demi Lovato had already met the Jonas Brothers before filming *Camp Rock* with them in Canada, but it was on set when rumors flew that she and her costar Joe Jonas were involved. Teen-magazine editors observed them acting all giggly while eating lunch together and disappearing into the camp's cabins to escape prying eyes.

"Of all the Jonas Brothers, Joe's the biggest flirt!" Alyson Stoner told *Twist* in January 2008 when asked about rumors of him and Demi. In the same article, Joe confessed, "Demi's voice is amazing."

In the January/February 2008 issue of *m*, Joe and Demi's status as a couple was officially given a big "maybe" by the editors! "We're here to tell you that while we were on the set, we witnessed some major chemistry between Joe and Demi with our own eyes."

Demi's BFF Selena Gomez admitted to *Twist* in April 2008, "They make each other laugh! Something might happen between them in the future!" Costar Alyson Stoner concurred, adding, "There were definitely on-set crushes!" Selena went on to say, "When Joe and Demi are together, they're awesome. They love being around each other. You can tell when they're together, there's chemistry there!"

When *Tiger Beat* asked Demi about rumors she was dating Joe, in its May 2008 issue, she replied, "Absolutely not! We are just friends. Joe is like a brother to me." (Keep in mind this is the same line Zac Efron and Vanessa Hudgens used before it became obvious they were definitely *not* like siblings!)

Interestingly, when Joe was asked by *Twist* if he got nervous before shooting his romantic scenes with Demi,

he said, "No, I was in the moment!"

Still, both Joe and Demi have insisted they've never been more than just friends. But can their friendship last without romance interfering?

Joe told *Bop* in May 2008 that girls and guys can be "just friends," no problem. "I have a good friend who's a girl. It's one of those relationships where maybe something will happen one day, maybe it won't. I don't want to move on anything because she's my good friend and I don't want to ruin our friendship. It would be awkward and weird."

Could he have been talking about . . . Demi Lovato?

THE CHELSEA STAUB SCANDAL!

"Can I just tell you that it's my New Year's resolution not to fall in love with any of the Jonas Brothers!" Chelsea Staub told *m* in its January/February 2008 issue. She was saying this because she'd been signed as the female lead on their TV show, then entitled *J.O.N.A.S.* (now just *JONAS*).

"I absolutely adore the Jonas Brothers!" Chelsea said to *J-14* in its May/June 2008 issue. "They're such great guys! We're really close. I can't get enough of their little brother Frankie!"

When paparazzi photos surfaced the following summer of Joe on what appeared to be a shopping date with Chelsea Staub—holding her hand!—fans needed the truth.

Nick came to his brother's defense, telling *Twist* in July 2008, "I think it's hilarious. They were just hanging out—sometimes me and Chelsea hang out, too! We're all good friends. Joe was being a gentleman by helping her into the elevator. It just goes to show that if you take a pic with someone, people will assume you're dating."

Do you see a pattern here? Remember, Joe was also holding JoJo's hand because she was in heels in the snow. Now he's holding Chelsea's hand because she's got shopping bags and is getting on an elevator.

But the denials sank in and no further photos of Joe hanging with Chelsea came out. Maybe it was just a summer romance?

"I had a summer relationship that was kind of funny. It was like one of those things [like] in the movie where it lasts over the summer and then it's over," Joe said to *Bop* in May 2008. "But it was fun!"

"It is difficult to maintain relationships with the kind of life we live."

TAYLOR SWIFT: A GIRL SCORNED!

In the May/June 2008 issue of *Twist*, Joe said the words every JoBros fan longs to hear: "We're all very single. We're on the road a lot. It gets crazy!"

But by the time they'd launched their Burning Up Tour, Joe was no longer single—he was very much involved with superstar country singer Taylor Swift. Fans aren't blind, so they were able to observe Joe sneaking into her shows to watch her from the soundboard and vice versa. Taylor even performed with the guys at a couple of shows, fanning the flames of gossip.

Don't ever try to fool a Jonas Brothers fan—one time, the guys posted a hilarious video on YouTube and fans noticed you could see part of a blonde girl's form in a mirror in one frame. Was it Taylor? No one can know for sure, but the probability was high.

Later, Joe and his brothers were caught red-handed with their girlfriends (Nick with Selena Gomez, Kevin with Danielle Deleasa) in New York City, marking one of the first times Joe had been photographed with Taylor.

"It's been awesome hanging with JB. People can say what they want about me and Joe," Taylor told *m*'s October/November 2008 issue.

But trouble was brewing—the Jonas Brothers don't like to be too public about the girls they're dating, and rumor has it that Taylor was fed up with the intrigue. She was also said to be sick of never seeing Joe.

"When we have girl-friends, we want to be there for them because we'll be thinking about them nonstop!" Joe told *m* in June 2008. "We always care a lot about the girls we date—even if we can't see them all the time!"

Shockingly, Joe wound up breaking things off with Taylor in what she openly described as a twenty-seven–second phone call. Big mistake!

Taylor's reaction was to speak publicly about the breakup in terms that made Joe look like a cad. She did an *On Air with Ryan Seacrest* interview in which Ryan asked if she'd "ever really been deeply hurt by anyone," to which Taylor said, "Once . . . You just have to realize that someday you'll find someone that's right for you." She went on to say that the reason she and Joe could never be seen in public was that the JoBros' management team forbade it, since they felt it would hurt Joe's bachelor image among his fans.

Taylor made a YouTube video with a Joe Jonas *Camp Rock* doll, saying, "See, this one even comes with a phone so he can break up with other dolls." At another time, she also hinted that Joe might have left her for another girl. One rumor involved Joe and fellow Disney Channel star Brenda Song of *The Suite Life on Deck*, but then photos surfaced of Joe and his crew on a Mexican holiday with glamorous actress Camilla Belle.

Joe hoped they could be friends one day, but knew it would take time. "My advice is you need time to get back to normal after a break-up," Joe said to *Twist*'s May/June 2008 issue. "You can't be like, 'I want to be BFF again' right away." Good thing this is Joe's theory, because "never" is a more likely time frame than "right away" when it comes to this particular ex!

To do a little damage control, Joe issued an unusual statement on the band's MySpace that asserted his right to privacy while defending his reputation. "Like all people our age we are trying to find someone special that we can share time with in our busy lives. . . . [But] it is difficult to maintain relationships with the kind of life we live." Joe went on to specifically address the accusations directed at him: "I never cheated on a girlfriend. It might make someone feel better to assume or imply I have been unfaithful but it is simply not true." Of the notoriously short call from Taylor, Joe said, "A phone call can be pretty short when someone else ends the call."

After making this point, the Jonas Brothers later mysteriously deleted the blog.

Only time will tell if Brenda or Camilla will be that "someone special," or if Joe will keep searching for the girl of his dreams!

KEVIN JONAS: SECRETS OF A GIRL MAGNET!

THE AWKWARD YEARS!

"I'm prone to finding someone who doesn't treat me well, but lucky enough to get away from them!" Kevin told *J-14* in February 2008.

Yikes! You would think someone like Kevin would never have girl troubles, and in truth, most of his issues are behind him. But when Kevin was younger, he had a harder time with girls than either of his brothers—which might be why he's so wise about them now.

Once in grade school, Kevin had a girlfriend who really knew how to make a guy feel bad—he told *m*'s January/February 2008 issue that she "would send back the notes I had written her with all my spelling errors circled. I would get so upset. I didn't want to look like an idiot!"

He also had a girlfriend in school who demanded a lot of his time and attention. "I spent a lot of time with my crush, like every day for about a year and a half," Kevin explained to *Bop* in its June/July 2008 issue. "I even sat through some school plays and talent shows to be with her." He told *Tiger Beat* in November 2006 that one play was so bad it gave him "such a headache by the end."

Kevin's awkwardness around girls ended around the same time his first serious relationship did. "I had a high school sweetheart," Kevin told *J-14* in February 2008. "We dated from thirteen until I was a junior in high school. Then, we broke up and that was it. Things changed over time because of what I'm doing now. I started going on the road and grew up a little more. She's an amazing girl, but that was my big growing-up crush."

Kevin grew up while seeing that girl, and never looked back—now, he's the girl go-to guy of the Jonas Brothers!

"I've always wanted to pick someone up at the airport and have a movie-esque kiss!"

DATING ADVICE FROM A BIG BROTHER!

You may think of Joe as the ultimate Jonas playa, but Joe told *Popstar!* in September 2006, "Kevin's like the *king* of romance, my gosh!" Being older, Kevin had more time to gather dating experiences. Both Joe and Nick still look to him for his advice on how to woo girls.

Kevin has a very trendy favorite type of food for first dates. "Sushi's good unless you're allergic to fish. Bad date food would be sloppy joes because it gets all over your clothes. You wouldn't want your date to think you're messy!" Kevin advised in *Bop* in May 2008.

In general, if you go out with Kevin, expect a relaxing time, not a crazy adventure (though he *does* love a good carnival). "I like very cool, very chill dates," Kevin told *Twist* in its May/June 2008 issue. "I love going to dinner and just hanging out in New York City or here in L.A.—just keep it low-key and have fun. Something really calm and chill is nice."

Kevin's a fan of New York's Little Italy. He told *Twist*'s September 2006 issue, "This is the best place to take a girl. At night, there's so many lights, and they put the tables in the middle of the street."

Lighting is key for Kevin! "I went to a little candlelit restaurant in New Jersey, and it was really cute," Kevin told *J-14* in the October/November 2008 issue. "It was fun. After dinner, we went and saw Christmas lights. It was awesome. It was a good first date."

But Kevin has grand visions for his dates, even if many wind up being low-key.

He told *Twist* in April 2008, "I've always wanted to pick someone up at the airport and have a movie-esque kiss!"

"It would be an amazing story if I met someone on vacation and ended up spending the rest of my life with her," Kevin told *J-14* in August 2008.

One of the best pieces of advice Kevin has doled out to his brothers—and that you might want to heed as well—involves the age-old problem of whether or not to date someone who's been a good friend.

"There's *always* so many risks in dating a friend . . . because you don't want to lose that friend later on if it doesn't work out," Kevin told *Fans' Choice: Jonas Brothers—Living the Dream!* "But if you can find a person that you're just friends with, then it's cool. And I'm sure you will end up dating at some point."

Well said!

WHAT K.JO LOOKS FOR IN A GIRL!

Kevin is the Jonas brother who is least often associated with mystery girlfriends, partly because he tends to date girls seriously for longer periods of time, and partly because even though he attracts girls right and left, he isn't always eager to start a relationship.

"Sometimes, guys need a good friend more than a girlfriend," Kevin told *m* in June 2007.

But when he's looking, Kevin has a long list of qualities that he finds attractive in a potential GF.

"I love a good smile," Kevin told *Bop* in April 2008. "It's also cool to have a nice conversation." Kevin is the most talkative Jonas; he used to serve as an unofficial publicist for them at photo shoots, schmoozing with the media because it was second nature for him. So it makes sense that he'd prefer a girl with the gift of gab!

Physically, Kevin's tastes are all over the map. His childhood crush was Danielle Fishel, who played Topanga on *Boy Meets World*, and his current long-time GF, Danielle Deleasa, is brunette, but he told *Bop* in December 2006, "I'm a sucker for blondes and redheads."

More along the lines of his preference for blondes, Kevin took the unusual step of publicly proclaiming a crush on Hilary Duff. Kevin made his public appeal for Hilary's heart in *m* in March 2008 saying, "I've been dying to meet Hilary for a long time. I think she's single now, so that's pretty awesome. I'd like to date her!"

Joe and Nick are the biggest comedians of the group, but Kevin has a real appreciation for humor. If you wanna get with Kevin, you should share this trait. In *J-14* in September 2008 he said, "Someone who can make you laugh and be okay with just talking on the phone for a while instead of seeing you!" when asked to describe his ideal GF.

He likes phone convos, but is also way into IMing. "The wink faces on the IMs are always good," Kevin told *J-14* in February 2008, proving that even if your BF is far away, there are ways to be affectionate.

Kevin explained to *J-14* in August 2008 why it's so impossible to date while on tour. "We've been in five states in three days. It's crazy sometimes." Along with being understanding of his tight sked and globe-trotting, you should try not to be overly fannish around Kevin if you hope to catch his eye.

Kevin told *Fans' Choice: Jonas Brothers—Living the Dream!*, "I'm attracted to someone that's totally and completely cool. . . . I really like it when they're not impressed. Or they put on the face of not impressed. So I'll be thinking, 'Wait, what, why are you this way? I have to find out!' One thing that's not attractive is when someone's like, 'Oh, hi, I totally like you!' There's no mystery there. From fans, it's great! But from girls that you're going to date, it's different."

Even though he's usually the one his brothers turn to for dating advice, Kevin relies on his bros, too. In the past, Kevin has fallen for only one girl who his brothers didn't like. "It ended terribly," he told *Tiger Beat* in May 2008. "They were right, and now I listen to everyone's advice." Because of that bad experience, he would never again date a girl his brothers disapproved of.

But they would never veto a girl who had the single most important quality.

"She needs to be loving and put others before herself," Kevin said of an ideal date-mate to *Tiger Beat* in May 2008.

KEVIN IN ACTION!

Kevin is no longer a newbie with girls, but he's also not overconfident. "When I'm around the girl I like, I sweat!" Kevin confessed to *Bop* in January 2008.

"I've learned not to rush into things

so quickly if I like someone," Kevin said in *Bop* in May 2008. "I don't practice what I say before I call my crush. That would be really lame."

But his charm is undeniable.

"Whenever I meet somebody, I always end up with her contact info in my Sidekick," he boldly told *Twist* in March 2007. The magazine decided he'd be a great match for JoJo—not so far off considering JoJo is already a good pal of the Jonas Brothers . . . although one who's reportedly dated Joe!

Ultimately, Kevin's demeanor when talking with girls is a reflection of his outlook on life—don't overthink it.

"I'm never sure of what I'm going to talk about. But once we're face-to-face, I'm good. I'm able to talk well in the moment," he said to *Twist* in March 2008.

KEVIN KNOWS HOW TO TREAT A LADY!

Once he's involved with a girl, Kevin is always a proper gentleman, and quite thoughtful regarding her happiness.

"I would make sure my girl was able to come to as many of my shows as possible. She has to be her own rock star!" Kevin said to *m* in July 2008.

So just because he's on tour, that doesn't mean he's off-limits. "I flew to see a girlfriend over Christmas once. I was on tour, so getting to see her for the holidays was fun," he reminisced with *Twist* in January 2008.

As a kid, Kevin was already honing his romantic skills. "When I had a girlfriend in school, we'd time it so that when I would

ask to go to the bathroom, she would go to the bathroom, too! We wouldn't cut class, but we'd be able to see each other in the hallway for a minute. It was cool!" Kevin told *Twist* in April 2008.

But the most romantic thing he ever did for a girl happened one Valentine's Day—and it was so amazing, little bro Joe later copied the same idea!

"I wrote a letter to a GF one V-day. Then I burnt the edges, rolled it up, put it in a bottle and sealed it with wax. Her mom put it in her room while she was sleeping, so it was waiting for her when she woke up," Kevin told *Twist* in February 2008.

Can you imagine receiving such a thoughtful Valentine's Day offering from any boy, let alone from Kevin Jonas?

BROTHERLY PACT!

"A girl needs to understand about brothers—we talk about *everything*," Kevin told *Twist* in March 2007. Take that as a word of warning, all you potential Jonas girlfriends . . . !

"Certain people are off-limits, like if there's some girl I liked in the past," Kevin told *J-14* in September 2008. Even among girls they've just met or seen for the first time—cute fans in the crowd—there is honor among Jonases! "Say there's a really pretty girl,

Kevin had this to say about East Coast vs. West Coast girls in *Popstar!* in November 2007: "In New York, wow . . . they're really different. We've been finding that out more and more! In New York, girls will keep walking. There's a whole different attitude. I can't explain it—it's like, I don't want to say it's too good for you, but she puts off almost as though you have to try a *lot* harder. We love them both, though!"

and you've been looking at her—and we've all noticed her—but at the end of the show, she holds up a 'Nick, I love you' sign, then it's, 'Okay, Nick, you win!'"

When Kevin met Lauren Conrad from *The Hills* at an awards show, he introduced himself and explained which band he was from. "Oh, I know," she said. "I'm a huge fan." Kevin told *m* in March 2008, "I was like, 'What?' So it was just *really* nice to meet her."

But as excited as Kevin was to meet Lauren, he knew that Joe was the one who'd always spoken of crushing on her—so he didn't ask Lauren out. (Although Joe didn't either . . . what kind of brother pact is that?)

NOT-SO-GREAT DATES!

Despite all the breaks he's gotten in life, Kevin has also had the two most common breaks of all—heartbreak and breakups. And yes, even Kevin Jonas has had bad breaks when it comes to girls and dating.

When asked by *Teen* for its Summer 2008 issue what really annoys him, Kevin grumpily wrote, "Ex-girlfriends," and admitted in *J-14* in August 2008 that the biggest dramas he's ever had were "break-ups. I've encountered heartbreak. There's always one where you break up with somebody and never talk to them."

Luckily, most of his dating disasters have been more momentary embarrassments. "I was dating this girl and . . . it was the worst. I kissed her and she had a hairy lip! I didn't say anything to her, but it was like, just go wax or something. It was terrible!" he told *Twist* in its May/June 2006 issue. Gross!

As much of a turnoff as a hairy lip is when a girl is with Kevin, but not really *with* him, "The most annoying thing a girl could do is text on her cell phone during the entire date," Kevin told *Twist* in February 2007.

But it's not always the girl's fault— Kevin is big enough to admit when he's screwed up!

Kevin told *Twist* in March 2008, "One time, I took this girl out to eat at a really nice place in L.A. We ordered a ton of food, but when the bill came, I realized I forgot my wallet at home! My dad had to come bring it to me. It was so embarrassing!"

When the date is over, make sure you let Kevin know if you want to see him again. "If we have to work too hard at it, it can be really annoying," Kevin told *J-14* in February 2008. "You just want to take a girl on a date, and she won't return phone calls until after you give up. What the heck? Games are not cool."

ZOE MYERS: KEVIN'S FIRST POST-FAME GF!

Back in July 2006, when "Year 3000" was just getting the Jonas Brothers some national attention, Kevin Jonas was about to go off the market.

According to *m* in April 2008, Kevin met Zoe Myers at the video shoot for "Year 3000," and then dated her for close to a year. Zoe, a beautiful brunette, was the lead pink-haired future girl in that quirky video. Alas, once fans caught wind of the association—Zoe had pictures posted on the Internet—the relationship ended.

"Kevin is very sweet. To me, he wasn't a 'Jonas Brother,' he was just Kevin. We spent a lot of time on the phone and flying across the country to see each other. The Jonas family is very special to me!" Zoe told *m* in a rare interview.

DANIELLE DELEASA: KEVIN'S SOUL MATE?

In the June 2008 issue of *Tiger Beat*, paparazzi photos were published showing the guys on a private Miami cruise. In one of the photos, Kevin's rumored GF Danielle was pictured, chatting with Joe. She was only identified as a "friend," but many hard-core fans knew this was a major revelation. Fans were already onto Danielle because she had been seen briefly in the guys' reality series *Living the Dream* on Disney Channel.

Danielle Deleasa grew up in Wyckoff, New Jersey, the same town the Jonas Brothers called home during their formative years. Fans have spotted Danielle at various JoBros shows, so it's very likely that she is the girl he was speaking of when *Twist* asked him about dating on the road.

"I was able to have a girl come to a show recently. I only saw her for like five minutes during the show, but we hung out backstage afterwards a little bit. It was cool!" Kevin confided to *Twist* in August 2008.

After photos popped up showing Kevin and Danielle shopping in Yorkville, fans' suspicions were further fanned.

Ryan Seacrest openly asked Kevin about Danielle live on his show, drawing a very terse reply from Kevin, who did not seem too pleased to have her name used. His nonanswer was answer enough—and fans have come to accept Danielle much more so than Nick's or Joe's more famous female friends.

In September 2008, the boys were seen at the chic restaurant Tao in Manhattan with Danielle, Selena, and Taylor, seemingly confirming the status of all three mystery relationships. But the final proof came in October 2008, when Kevin and Danielle were photographed shopping and making out in Brentwood. Kevin even took a pic of them kissing with his own camera!

What is it about Danielle that makes her a good match for Kevin? Along with a shared history, one safe bet is that Danielle is probably very understanding of Kevin's career considerations.

Kevin told *Twist* in September 2008, "I want a girl I can talk to on the phone, and it be okay that I'm not always there."

what would your ideal jonas date be?

START

Are you low- or high-maintenance?

LOW   **HIGH**

Can you swim?

YES

Do you prefer to be outdoors or indoors?

IN   **OUT**

NO

Do you like chilling out or being active?

ACTIVE

CHILLING

Is it okay for a girl to win a game vs. her BF?

OF COURSE   **BAD IDEA**

Are you a picky eater, or will you eat anything?

ANYTHING

PICKY

Nonstop fun or quiet bonding?

BONDING   **FUN**

Sporty or lazy?

SPORTY   **LAZY**

DINNER & A MOVIE!
Your perfect date with a JoBro would be joining one of them for some great food (they always have to eat on the run) and a hilarious movie at the multiplex. Hint: Joe loves Will Ferrell!

GOLFING & GO-KARTING!
The only way to go for you would be an active date—Nick loves golfing and both of his bros like mini golf, or you could try go-karting to prove you're a girl who's one of the boys!

BEACHIN' IT!
If you get your chance to spend time with a Jonas, pick out the cutest swimsuit ever and head to the water! Beach dates are great for conversation and physical activity . . . plus, have you seen Kevin in shorts?

154

THE JOBROS' FIRST KISSES!

NICK!

Nick, in his own handwriting, reported to *Teen* in Summer 2008 that his first kiss was, "Awesome!" It's possible that Nick's first kiss was with Miley Cyrus, who said in *Twist* in December 2007, "My first kiss was really good. It was looking over the city skyline. It was sweet! It was awesome." When asked if Nick was the guy kissing her, she replied, "Umm, maybe, but uh, maybe not!"

KEVIN!

Kevin told Teen in Summer 2008 that his first peck was "Awful. Well, it was just not perfect." But by the time he was being interviewed by *Fans' Choice: Jonas Brothers—Living the Dream!* just a month or so later, he said, "You know, this is terrible, but I can't fully remember exactly when my first kiss was! It was a long time ago. It was just like a kiss—it was like, 'Okay, *there*, you!'"

JOE!

"My first kiss was at camp!" Joe blurted out to *Fans' Choice: Jonas Brothers—Living the Dream!* "It just kind of happened—we kissed and then we went to join everyone else and ate lunch. It was kind of like, 'Okay, we kissed.' We were there for four days and then didn't really need to say anything to each other. I think we both knew it was just a camp thing!"

Joe remembered this first smooch as "Great!" when asked by *Teen* in Summer 2008. His advice on first kisses? "Close your eyes," he told *Twist* in July 2008. That way, he said, "You know it's real. It's almost like a Disney movie!"

155

Jonas Brothers Evolution!

EARLY 2005 Signed to Columbia as a group.

DECEMBER 27, 2005 "Mandy" is released—their first-ever single!

JANUARY 2006 First appearance in a national magazine—*Popstar!* They're called "Break-Out Stars of 2006" along with Alyson Stoner, Hawk Nelson, and Josh Hutcherson.

MARCH 1, 2006 The JoBros appear on TRL to introduce their three-part "Mandy" video! "Two for me is the best video because it's most cliffhanger-ish," Kevin later told *Popstar!* in July 2006.

JULY 22, 2006 The Radio Disney 10th Anniversary Concert attracts a multitude of huge Disney stars, including newcomers the Jonas Brothers. Joe later told *Popstar!* in June 2007 of an embarrassing moment for the band: "We always spray fans with things because they give us all this party stuff at concerts, like silly string and confetti. When we did Radio Disney's 10th birthday concert, I was going to spray the fans, but instead I didn't know where the nozzle was and it was actually on me. So I was spraying myself the whole time!"

AUGUST 8, 2006 *It's About Time* is finally released (and it really is about time)!

OCTOBER/NOVEMBER 2006 *Twist* openly speculates on a possible Miley Cyrus and Nick Jonas hookup!

LATE FALL 2006 Boo-hoo! The Jonas Brothers are dropped by Columbia Records!

JANUARY 2007 First appearance (at #10) on *J-14*'s "Hottest in Rock" poll!

FEBRUARY 8, 2007 Hollywood Records announces they are "delighted" to have signed the Jonas Brothers and Topps Confections also announces a Jonas partnership to help sell Baby Bottle Pop candies.

FEBRUARY 20, 2007 The guys are surprise guests at the album-release party for labelmates Everlife!

FEBRUARY 20, 2007 **The Jonas Brothers are the subject of their first major *Billboard* article**

MARCH 9, 2007 **They play a "thank you" concert for their old school, Eastern Christian High.**

MARCH 11, 2007 **The Jonases attend Carnival for a Cure, a diabetes charity event, at which Nick announces to the world he has been diagnosed with type 1 diabetes.**

APRIL 2007 **They go on tour, opening for Jesse McCartney!**

APRIL 13, 2007 **When the Jonas Brothers open for JMac in Boca Raton, Florida, most of the audience leaves before Jesse performs.**

APRIL 26, 2007 **The guys appear at their first Disney Channel Games!**

MAY 5, 2007 **The Jonases join the Bamboozle Festival, along with Cute Is What We Aim For and Drop Dead, Gorgeous.**

MAY 9, 2007 **Disney Channel announces it is ordering up a pilot for a new Jonas Brothers sitcom called *J.O.N.A.S.***

JUNE 2, 2007 **The guys make a hugely successful appearance at Six Flags Magic Mountain in Valencia, California, with a surprise introduction by Miley Cyrus! Pictures of the boys riding rides with Miley—and of Miley with her armsflung around Nick's waist— led to lots of fan chatter about "Niley"!**

JUNE 18, 2007 **The JoBros film their "S.O.S." video on the *Queen Mary*.**

JUNE 25, 2007 **Kickoff of their first headlining tour of theaters, clubs, and fairs. Some of their audiences have over 1,000 fans.**

JUNE 27, 2007 **First White House visit!**

JULY 18, 2007 ***Jonas Brothers* is announced as their second CD, and it's revealed the record will be the first to take advantage of CDVU+ technology!**

AUGUST 2007 **The Bros make a big impact at the 6th Annual *Popstar!* Poptastic Awards, winning Poptastic Group or Duo, Song, and Ringtone!**

AUGUST 7, 2007 **Their second CD, *Jonas Brothers*, is released!**

AUGUST 8, 2007 **Their uncle Josh proposes to his GF during "Please Be Mine" at the New York City show!**

AUGUST 15, 2007 ***Jonas Brothers* debuts at #5 on *Billboard*!**

AUGUST 17, 2007 **The Jonas episode of *Hannah Montana*, "Me and Mr. Jonas and Mr. Jonas and Mr. Jonas," airs to stellar ratings!**

AUGUST 24, 2007 **The guys sing "Hold On" and "S.O.S." on *Miss Teen USA*!**

AUGUST 26, 2007 **The guys bring their mom Denise as their "date" to Teen Choice 2007! Fans go ape as the Jonases take the stage alongside Miley Cyrus, who announces their upcoming shared tour!**

SEPTEMBER 12, 2007 **Disney Channel announces the start of filming on *Camp Rock*!**

SEPTEMBER 27, 2007 **J.O.N.A.S. officially gets the "green light"—meaning it's approved—by Disney Channel. (Shocking how long the process took, right?)**

OCTOBER 9, 2007 **The Jonases join Ashanti in announcing the nominees for the American Music Awards.**

OCTOBER 16, 2007 **"I Wanna Be Like You" is covered by the Jonas Brothers on the DVD of *The Jungle Book*!**

OCTOBER 18, 2007 **Miley's Best of Both Worlds Tour kicks off with the JoBros as her opening act.**

OCTOBER 30, 2007 ***Jonas Brothers: The Bonus Jonas Edition* is released!**

NOVEMBER 13, 2007 **The guys are honored at the *CosmoGIRL!* Born to Lead Awards.**

NOVEMBER 22, 2007 **The guys appear on the Build-a-Bear float at the Macy's Thanksgiving Day Parade, belting out "S.O.S."**

NOVEMBER 23, 2007 **The boys give a huge *Good Morning America* performance!**

DECEMBER 14, 2007 ***Jonas Brothers* goes platinum!**

DECEMBER 14, 2007 **The guys perform at Z100's Jingle Ball in New York City!**

DECEMBER 31, 2007 **JoBros and Miley sing "We Got the Party" for *Dick Clark's New Year's Rockin' Eve*!**

JANUARY 2008 **Live Nation signs the band to a two-year, megabucks touring deal!**

JANUARY 18, 2008 **The guys meet up with Miley Cyrus again at the red-carpet premiere of the *Hannah Montana/Miley Cyrus: Best of Both Worlds Concert Tour* movie!**

JANUARY 31, 2008 **The guys launch their Look Me in the Eyes Tour.**

FEBRUARY 2008 **They perform in Houston, Texas, at their very first sold-out arena for 14,000 fans! "We looked out at the audience and started laughing," Kevin remembered. "There were just so many people, and they were all looking at us. It was complete joy."**

FEBRUARY 19, 2008 **Chevy Rocks the Future event, kicking off the JoBros' involvement in environmental issues.**

FEBRUARY 22, 2008 **Breakfast Breaks concert at Kimball Middle School in Elgin, Illinois!**

MARCH 1, 2008 **ChangeForTheChildren.com goes live with JB, matching dollar-for-dollar, the first $10,000 raised!**

MARCH 22, 2008 **Handprint ceremony at Planet Hollywood-Times Square!**

MARCH 24, 2008 **George W. Bush welcomes the Jonas Brothers to sing "The Star-Spangled Banner" at the White House Easter Egg Roll.**

MARCH 25, 2008 **Covering a-ha's '80s hit "Take On Me," the boys razzle-dazzle 'em on *Dancing with the Stars*!**

MARCH 29, 2008 **Guess who won Best Music Group at this year's Kids' Choice Awards?**

APRIL 8, 2008 **The JoBros invade the UK for photo shoots, radio interviews, and concerts!**

APRIL 17, 2008 **A promo tour to Mexico is a huge hit! "Mexico was crazy!" Kevin told *Popstar!* in August 2008. "We had such a great time. We played for 80,000 people on the first night. It was a radio show, but every single day just got better and better. We learned so much about the culture and the food and we cannot wait to go back!"**

APRIL 23, 2008 The JoBros make a surprise appearance at Ricardo Lizarraga Elementary School in Los Angeles in celebration of Earth Day!

APRIL 26, 2008 Surprise! The Jonas Brothers show up at the White House Correspondents' Dinner.

APRIL 27, 2008 The guys fly down to Orlando to begin filming—and competing in!—the annual Disney Channel Games!

MAY 21, 2008 The guys perform on the *American Idol* finale.

JUNE 14, 2008 The *Camp Rock* soundtrack premieres on Radio Disney.

JUNE 20, 2008 *Camp Rock* premieres on Disney Channel. It's also playing on ABC, ABC Family, and Disney.com!

JULY 4, 2008 The Burning Up Tour kicks off in Toronto, Canada, featuring Demi Lovato as the opening act!

JULY 23, 2008 The first-ever Jonas *Rolling Stone* cover goes on sale!

JULY 24, 2008 The first-ever Jonas *Forbes* cover goes on sale, and they're dubbed "teen titans" for all their wealth and success.

AUGUST 2008 The JoBros win huge at the *Popstar!* Poptastic Awards, taking home thirteen trophies!

AUGUST 10, 2008 The boys begin a three-night, sold-out stand at Madison Square Garden in New York City.

AUGUST 12, 2008 *A Little Bit Longer* hits stores!

AUGUST 18, 2008 The guys get their own wax figures at Madame Tussaud's!

AUGUST 20, 2008 Joe receives his high-school diploma onstage in Atlanta!

AUGUST 22, 2008 The Jonas Brothers donate the suits they wore on the cover of *A Little Bit Longer* to the Rock 'n' Roll Hall of Fame!

SEPTEMBER 29, 2008 Finally! The newly retitled *JONAS* (instead of *J.O.N.A.S.*) begins shooting in Los Angeles!

NOVEMBER 8, 2008 The boys perform on the *Kristi Yamaguchi & Friends* TV special!

NOVEMBER 24, 2008 The Jonas Brothers host a launch party in L.A. for their first-ever book, *Burning Up: On Tour with the Jonas Brothers!*

JANUARY 19, 2009 The Jonases, Miley Cyrus, Demi Lovato, Bow Wow, and Keke Palmer appeared at the Kids' Inaugural Concert in celebration of the swearing-in of President Barack Obama.

JANUARY 21, 2009 Miley Cyrus posts a video at MileyWorld.com in which she says, "I love Nicky."

FEBRUARY 6, 2009 The JoBros perform at a Neil Diamond tribute concert.

FEBRUARY 8, 2009 The guys realize a lifelong dream by performing a medley of "Burnin' Up" and "Superstition" with the legendary Stevie Wonder at the Grammys. (Did you notice Nick messed up a few words? Oops!)

FEBRUARY 14, 2009 JoBros rock *Saturday Night Live!*

FEBRUARY 22, 2009 Nick, Kevin, and Joe are interviewed by Barbara Walters as part of her annual pre–Oscar show.

FEBRUARY 27, 2009 *Jonas Brothers: The 3D Concert Experience* opens in movie theaters and on IMAX screens across America!

Jonas Style!

Everyone thinks of the Jonas Brothers as the most stylish young men in Hollywood— but their fashion sense has definitely evolved with the help of their beloved stylist Michelle Tomaszewski, with whom they're rumored to be developing a clothing line.

The Jonas Brothers were in polos and pastels before they met their stylist Michelle Tomaszewski. It was Michelle who cooked up their dandy rock star look and who opened them up to designer brands. The guys have always given her credit for her work. "They needed help putting elegance back into dressing for guys," she told *People*. Michelle has also been the stylist for Demi Lovato.

Check out their guy getups over the years!

Ed Hardy T-shirts and distressed jeans were in style with the Jonas Brothers throughout 2006!

"I'll wear a shirt once or twice and I can't wear it again," Kevin admitted in *Twist*'s October/November 2006 issue.

"It's green and it's like a T-ball shirt. I love my vintage clothes," Kevin admitted to *Bop* in June/July 2007 of his favorite article of clothing. "It's the first shirt I ever bought when I went to a Salvation Army, so that was really cool."

Kevin is not afraid of almost any color or style. In September 2006, he proudly posed in a bubblegum-pink Ed Hardy tee, saying, "Pink is definitely the best. Real men wear pink."

By 2007, the guys were experimenting with more offbeat styles, including matching a vintage tuxedo jacket with a trendy tee. They also came to be known for wearing supertight pants!

"Style is a really big thing for us," Joe told *People*, "so every day we dress up and put on ties and wear J. Lindeberg and Marc Jacobs. We love to put on a high-fashion rock look. The only sweatpants I have are Adidas Velour."

"My best date outfit includes my zebra tie or my Hong Kong Mr. Lee custom-made suit and Dior shoes," Joe told *Tiger Beat* in March 2008. "When I get ready, I steal some things from Kevin's closet, maybe a little from Nick."

"Not only is it important to us to respect a girl, but to respect ourselves," Joe revealed to *J-14* in December 2007. "We want to be presented in a way that is not sloppy or anything like that."

As the guys got older, they began working ties and sweaters into their wardrobe for a punky/preppy look!

"People give us clothes to wear, which is really cool," Nick told *Popstar!* in October 2007. "It's like, 'Free clothes!' I haven't actually purchased any clothes in about a year. We're blessed!"

Kevin's desire to be stylish dates back to middle school. "I walked into class and every guy in the room had the same shirt," he told *Tiger Beat* in October 2008. "I didn't like that so I tried not to let it happen again."

Joe's most famous signature look would have to be his red pants! He's worn them to several photo shoots and onstage for the Best of Both Worlds Tour. "I wouldn't say those red pants are his favorite," his mom Denise told *m* in its January/February 2008 issue. "He just has the ability to wear colors well because of his dark hair. When he was young, he loved wearing purple clothes!" Unlike Kevin, apparently, who when asked by *Tiger Beat* in May 2007 if he ever had any outfits his mom loved but he hated, replied, "Oh, you have no idea! I had these purple jeans—purple! And she made me wear them!"

Nick's famous red sunglasses were given to him by *Hannah Montana* cast member Moises Arias when the brothers filmed their highly rated appearance on that show.

Joe told *CosmoGIRL!* In Summer 2008, "Shoes and sunglasses are my favorite things in my wardrobe. I like crazy frames, especially gold and silver ones. I like shiny jackets. I want my clothes to pop out. I'm not afraid to wear bright colors."

Joe told *Bop* in April 2008 that a girl's sense of style can sometimes be what first attracts him to her "if it's really cool and hip." He thinks hats are a great way to get a guy's attention, saying, "We'll remember stuff like that." Good news for Selena Gomez, who told *Twist* in April 2008, "I really love their style, and I love wearing guys' shirts."

163

The Jonas Brothers' most famous look to date is their "modern dandy" look, as crafted by stylist Michelle Tomaszewski, characterized by jackets, velvet caps, ascots, and boots!

"I'm most comfortable wearing a tie and a T-shirt," Nick told *CosmoGIRL!* in Summer 2008. "And if I'm going out, I'll throw on a button-down shirt with a cool jacket. I'm a big watch guy. I love them!"

"Through all the past photo shoots, we've been able to acquire most of the clothing," Kevin told *Tiger Beat* in March 2008. "We've actually turned our living room into a wardrobe fitting room. I can't wait to come out with my own fashion line."

Kevin definitely loves clothes. "I'm the one who will look at a piece of clothing and tell you who the designer is," Kevin told *Life Story* in Winter 2008.

groom at the top!

If there is one part of the JoBros' look that girls have the strongest feelings about, it's their hair! When the guys first began performing, all three wore their hair very short, but they've each experimented with it over the years.

"My hair actually used to be straight," Nick revealed to *Tiger Beat* in March 2008, on the all-consuming topic of his hair. "When I turned twelve, my hair got curly. It was the weirdest thing in the world. It's always been kind of long. When it gets really long I want to cut it all off. My mom, dad and manager are always like, 'You have to keep your long hair.' Joe might be the one to dye his hair a crazy color, maybe even Kevin, but not me."

When Nick Jonas cut his hair recently, some fans were relieved and others immediately missed their shaggy idol. Kevin told *Tiger Beat* in September 2008 that it happened with very little planning. "He woke up one morning and went, 'I need to cut my hair, guys.'"

"I spend five or ten minutes on my hair," Joe told *Twist* in August 2008. "Kevin takes the longest!"

Kevin's also got the curliest hair of the three—it takes up to forty-five minutes to straighten his naturally curly hair. According to their one-time groomer, Kevin uses Phyto Pro products on his hair and Kiehl's creative wax for control. The look he's going for is the "aristocratic rock star," while Joe's hair is supposed to suggest "Japanese anime," and Nick's hair and clothes are the "disheveled student" look.

"You would totally see us in things like a blazer and tie when we're not onstage," Kevin told *Bop* in its June/July 2008 issue. "That was part of our goals. We always said we wanted to bring some high fashion back to rock 'n' roll."

Kevin said to *CosmoGIRL!* in the Summer 2008 issue, "I love boots. Dark patent-leather ones are so sleek. I try to find them in vintage stores so no one else will have the same pair. Vests pairs with dress shirts, scarves, or suspenders are the best. When you like something, push the limits. Try layering and put different styles together. Combining is beautiful."

The guys' fave stores are Opening Ceremony and Scout, and they love Marc Jacobs and Dior.

HOW TO DRESS FOR THE JONAS BROTHERS!

"If she's a total prep, it's cool," Kevin said to *Twist* in April 2007.

"Leggings are awesome!" Joe said.

"She's got to take care of herself—no sweats!" was Nick's demand.

165

giving
back!

April 22, 2008 Date

Pay to
The Order of **TreePeople** $250,000

Two-hundred and fifty thousand dollars ——no/00 Dollars

Memo LA Million Trees

04222008:: 1774110:8003

"We play shows in hospitals and a bunch of the kids come out, sit in the front row and get so pumped," Kevin told *Tiger Beat* in September 2008. "It's really sweet."

"We want to cry when we meet people with stories—they're going through chemotherapy and things and they have a smile on their face, so happy, and you're, like, ready to cry. It makes us sad, but it also makes us happy," Joe said in *Popstar!* in October 2008.

For the guys, giving back is key. Without helping others, they could not enjoy their hard-earned success.

Because of their desire to help, the JoBros started the Change for the Children Foundation. "I think one of the most important things for us is that we wanted to have the kids have a say in what they choose, because . . . when you feel like you're a part of something because you made a decision, it means a whole lot!" the guys said.

"We just tell people to start saving the environment one step at a time."

"We want to be able to be a positive influence," Kevin said in *Popstar!* in October 2008.

One of their most passionate causes involves encouraging kids to go green.

"We have the Chevy Tahoe Hybrid," Kevin told *Popstar!* in October 2008. "We're very, very excited about that and we just tell people to start saving the environment one step at a time. We do that especially as a band, you know, with our album packaging. It's made out of 100% recyclable material [aside from] the CD itself."

Nick told *Popstar!* in October 2008, "Just do your best to recycle and, you know, really, really [make] an effort to do it."

Kevin advised in the same *Popstar!* issue, "Turn off the lights after you're done, unplug your TVs, unplug your computers when you're done using them. Even though they're plugged in and 'off,' they're still actually using energy and power, so those are little things that no one really thinks about."

167

JoBros A to Z

A

AIR DRUMS: Nick sometimes plays imaginary drums, which leads to quizzical looks! "I'll be standing at our meet-and-greets playing the air drums, and it actually makes sense in my head what I'm playing. But to everyone else, it just looks like I'm flinging my arms and spazzing out," Nick told *J-14* in December 2007.

AMERICAN MUSIC AWARDS: Held on Sunday, November 18, 2007, this was the awards show where Joe Jonas took a major tumble! The guys were singing "S.O.S." and the gimmick was they would emerge from behind panels of shattering glass. Unfortunately, clumsy Joe tripped and fell on the glass, bloodying his hand. Asked how he was able to go on with the performance, he told *J-14* in March 2008, "Just a little blood. Whatever, rock and roll!"

B

BABY BOTTLE POP: The boys endorsed this treat in mid-2007!

BACKSTREET BOYS: The Jonas Brothers opened for the ultimate boy band in 2005. Nick told *Popstar!* in January 2006 that he was paid a very high compliment by Brian Littrell. "Brian said, 'You're a lot like me, Nicholas!' and his wife even said, 'Brian, it's you!'"

BALONEY SANDWICHES: The family-friendly name of a card game that's all about bluffing, this was what the Jonas Brothers played on tour with Jesse McCartney. "We beat him in cards, but don't tell anybody!" they joked in *Popstar!* in January 2006.

BAND: Unlike so many guy groups that have become teen idols over the years, the Jonas Brothers actually write, play, and sing their own material. Still, they could not achieve the big sound they have live without a professional backing band—and they have one of the best in the biz! Currently, the band consists of John Taylor on guitar, Greg "Garbo" Garbowsky on bass guitar, Jack "Flawless" Lawless on drums and percussion, and Ryan Liestman on keyboards. All the guys are very familiar to die-hard fans, but Garbo—cute enough to be a teen pinup himself—has become especially well known thanks to his classic personal blog Let's Go on Tour. Sadly, he seems to have ceased blogging in June 2008 . . . probably because it became awkward writing about life on the road without accidentally revealing his employers'/friends' secrets!

BIG BERTHA: "Two years ago, we were in a big red passenger van with a trailer hitched to the back with all our gear," Nick said to *Rolling Stone* in 2008. That red van was affectionately nicknamed "Big Bertha." Joe remembered her having "a dent in it, and we'd flip the seats around and call it—" "The Players Lounge," Nick finished for him.

BIG ROB: The world's most famous bodyguard, Big Rob has been at the JoBros' side since 2006, after leaving the employ of Britney Spears. Rob has been in charge of protecting the guys when their fans get a little carried away, and yet he has become a fan favorite himself . . . so much so that he rapped in the band's music video for their hit single "Burnin' Up." Rob is not all brawn and no brains—he's very witty! Once, when a paparazzo asked the guys, "Which one of you fell at the American Music Awards?" Big Rob shot back, "We were just break-dancing."

BONUS JONAS: Little bro Frankie was

dubbed "the Bonus Jonas" by *Popstar!* Since then, the boys have taken the name and run with it—they even dubbed a re-release of their *Jonas Brothers* CD *The Bonus Jonas Edition!*

BOY BANDS: The Jonas Brothers are not technically a boy band, even if they are a band of boys! They're a proper pop/rock band in that they all play instruments as opposed to stressing dancing. But did you know Nick Jonas was once a boy band fanatic? "I was obsessed with boy bands!" he gushed in the May/June 2006 issue of *Twist*. Little did he know posters of him would wind up on just as many bedroom walls as posters of Justin Timberlake or Nick Carter!

BREAKFAST BREAKS: In 2008, the guys endorsed this healthy boxed breakfast that comes with cereal, juice, and a snack. (Nick's fave? The ones with Cinnamon Toast Crunch.) "We're on the road a lot, and need to stay energized, so we know how important breakfast is," Kevin explained to *Twist* in April 2008. "We have a different kind of stay-awake schedule, so I think it's important that you have nutrients that [are] able to keep [you] going in the morning," he added in *Fans' Choice: Jonas Brothers—Living the Dream!* The famous commercial showing them in "their" house was actually filmed at a rented home in Cincinnati, Ohio. Visit Breakfastbreaks.com for more info.

BUTTERFINGER: Kevin's all-time favorite candy bar!

CHICK FLICKS: Asked by *J-14* in July 2007 which chick flicks they secretly enjoy, Nick and Kevin went with *The Notebook* and Joe said, "*The Holiday* was a good movie."

CHORES: Part of the reason the guys are so down-to-earth is their parents' insistence on doing chores. In *Bop* in March 2007, Joe said, "We definitely have to do chores. We all help around the house. Taking out the trash is a big one. We have tons of bags."

CLOTHES: The guys *do* share clothes sometimes (but never socks!). "But if we borrow them, we'll remind each other to give it back!" Nick told *m* in July 2007.

CODE NAMES: Was Joe kidding around when he told *Tiger Beat* in September 2007 that their code names for each other in public are "Thunder Bolt, Lighting Bolt and Fierce Tiger"?

COLLEGE: So far, the boys have no concrete plans to attend college. Nick told *Popstar!* in March 2008, "Right now, I'm just enjoying the band, and if it continues to be great for us, I don't think I'll be going to college."

COLORS: The guys' fave colors, according to *Tiger Beat* in July 2006, are green (Kevin), dark blue (Nick), and blue (Joe).

COSTELLO, ELVIS: Nick worships this serious rock artist, and *Rolling Stone* brought the two together for a meeting of the minds in its October 30, 2008, issue. Costello was impressed by Nick, calling him "thoughtful and curious," and Nick asked his idol tons of questions about his career. After their meeting ended and Costello left, Nick was said to have "nodded his head a couple of times and said simply, 'That was *awesome.*'"

CREAM PIES: Joe insisted that various cream pies be available during meals while the guys were on their Burning Up Tour!

D

DAD: After the Jonas Brothers themselves, probably the most familiar face from their entourage to fans is that of Paul Kevin Jonas—their omnipresent dad. Kevin Sr. (like his son, he's never called Paul) has a tight bond with his sons personally and professionally, guiding them in life to become responsible adults, as well as steering their careers with as much savvy as any music manager. Without their dad, the boys would not be where they are today—his love of secular music is what encouraged them into the field, his financial support is what allowed them to pursue it full-time, and his creative vision (and respect for their own) is why they are one of the top acts in the world. Kevin Sr. is a respected leader not because he barks orders—he never does—but because his choices have proved wise over time and his authority as their father and spiritual mentor has never been challenged. When he's mad at his sons, instead of yelling, he just tells them he's "disappointed" . . . and that makes them a lot sorrier and a lot less likely to repeat an offense than if he'd made a bigger deal out of it!

DICAPRIO, LEONARDO: **One of Joe's most embarrassing moments ever relates to the** *Titanic* **superstar! "I was at a premiere party and Leonardo DiCaprio was there,"** Joe told *Tiger Beat* in December 2006. **"And I was talking to him, but I didn't know it was him! I was like, 'Hey, man! Who are you?' I went up to him later and apologized."**

DREAMS: **In one of their first substantial appearances in** *Bop*, **in December 2006, the boys were asked about weird dreams they'd had. Kevin described watching** *Gilligan's Island* **and** *Jurassic Park* **one day and then dreaming that a T. rex was eating Gilligan; Joe dreamed of Avril Lavigne stalking him; and Nick reported "a series of dreams in which I was a spy and I was doing crazy stuff. It was really funny because I kept having the dream for, like, four nights in a row."**

DUFF, HILARY: **The Jonas Brothers live close to the former Disney Channel star in L.A., but their affection for her is from afar. "I can't wait to finally meet Hilary Duff!"** Kevin told *Twist* in January 2008. **"It's such a funny story. I've never met her and we live like a block away from each other!"**

E

ELEPHANT: **Asked by** *Twist* **August 2008 what he wanted for his nineteenth birthday, Joe blurted out, "I want an elephant for my b-day!"** (He, uh, didn't get one!)

EMBARRASSMENT: **When something embarrassing happens in class, Nick's advice (in** *Tiger Beat* **in March 2008) is to "just laugh it off. [But] it's probably not the best thing to laugh in front of your teacher or they'll just embarrass you more! Just keep it cool until you get out of class, then play it up with your friends."**

EVERLIFE: **The Jonas Brothers are great friends of this Christian pop band. Labelmates, they showed up for Everlife's CD-release party in the spring of 2007, where they were photographed presenting Amber, Sarah, and Julia with long-stemmed red roses.**

F

FANS: **Everyone knows that the Jonas Brothers have the most devoted fans in the business. They built friendships with their fans through their famous meet-and-greets at all their early shows and via their constantly updated MySpace page. "Our fans are amazing,"** Kevin told *Bop* in December 2007. **"They'll drive across the country, stand outside until who knows when. We appreciate everything the fans do."** Nick added, **"We would be** *nowhere* **without them."** Sometimes, rumors circulate that the guys don't like doing meet-and-greets anymore—but that's not true! They've always loved them, as evidenced by Joe's comments in *Bop* in March 2008: **"It's exciting for us to meet our fans. We love hearing stories about how our music has influenced or changed their lives."** The only reason they've cut back on meet-and-greets is a lack of time.

FOUR KINGS GOLFING SOCIETY: According to Nick in *Tiger Beat* in November 2007, this was a little club consisting of Nick, Joe, and two members of their band.

FRECKLES: Kevin has freckles in the shape of a star on his neck.

G

GIRLS ALOUD: Kevin has said that he has crushes on the lovely ladies in this British pop group.

GRAMMYS: The guys received their first Grammy nomination in late 2008 as Best New Artist, along with Adele, Duffy, Lady Antebellum, and Jazmine Sullivan. It was controversial, since these "new" artists had released three albums since 2006!

GREEN: The guys are very involved in environmental issues and are always urging people to "go green." To this end, they're partnered up with Chevy and have filmed many spots to help influence kids in this direction. They also own a Chevrolet Tahoe 2 Mode Hybrid SUV, which was named the "green car of the year"!

GUITAR HERO: Kevin is a big fan of the game, which he considers to be a great way for kids to be exposed to a musical instrument!

H

HANSON: Especially when they were first starting out, the Jonas Brothers were often compared to this blond trio of rockin' bros. "We grew up with Hanson and they're unbelievable artists and writers!" they told *Popstar!* in January 2006.

HARVEST PARTY: In 1997, Joe went to that October's harvest party (a conservative-Christian alternative to the sometimes frowned-upon celebration of Halloween) as Grandpa from the religious series *Veggie Tales*, while Kevin went as the board game Operation and Nick went as Blue from the Nickelodeon show *Blue's Clues*. (When he was younger, Joe's favorite seasonal costume was as a bull rider atop a blow-up bull!) In general, the guys are big fans of dressing up—just check out their YouTube videos!

HIGH SCHOOL MUSICAL: Did you know that Kevin Jonas was *HSM*'s #1 fan? Back in May 2006, he confessed to *Twist*, "I don't know why, but I'm obsessed." In 2007, the guys and the cast of *Camp Rock* dressed up as the cast of *HSM* for Halloween in L.A.!

HILTON, PEREZ: The guys told *CosmoGIRL!*, "We knew we had made it when we were on Perez Hilton." The often nasty Internet gossip is a huge JoBros fan and has even interviewed the boys for his popular site!

HIPPO: A fan once adopted a hippo on behalf of the guys by donating money to a wildlife reserve. Would you believe that hippo's name is Jonas Brothers?

I

ICE CREAM: In *Tiger Beat* in July 2006, the boys said their fave flavors were rocky road (Kevin), cotton candy (Nick), and chocolate marshmallow (Joe).

J

JOBS: The guys told *J-14* in its October/November 2008 issue that if they weren't famous, their jobs would be "something with sports" (Nick), working at Starbucks (Kevin), and . . . the captain of a pirate ship (who else? Joe!).

JOEHAWK: Not a mohawk, not even a fauxhawk, but a Joehawk—this insider fan term refers to the look of Joe Jonas's hairstyle when he used to wear it short on the sides but spiky on the top.

JOHN'S PIZZA: This West Village restaurant, located at 278 Bleecker Street in Manhattan, is the guys' favorite pizza parlor.

K

KARDASHIAN, KIM: The racy reality-TV star went on the record as having a big crush on little Nick Jonas ("I don't think Reggie will get mad because Nick is like fifteen!"), which Nick loved hearing. He told *J-14* in August 2008, "That was awesome! I had bragging rights for about a day-and-a-half with my brothers. I was like, 'See this?' and Joe was like, 'Yes, you showed us five times!' And I was like, 'Well, just look at it again real quick!' It was pretty funny."

L

LA MELA RISTORANTE: One of the Bros' fave Italian restaurants is this family-style eatery in New York's Little Italy. Check it out at 167 Mulberry Street the next time you're in Manhattan, or visit Lamelarestaurant.com!

M

MACARONI AND CHEESE: Nick told *Twist* in September 2008 that his hidden talent is making "really good" mac 'n' cheese!

MATCHMAKER: Joe is an amazing match-maker! He once told bandmate Greg Garbowsky that a girl walking down the street was a good match for him. They chased her into a shopping area and finally caught up with her. Joe invited her shop-ping and she wound up joining them—and going to see a movie with Garbo!

MOCHI ICE CREAM: Joe is a huge fan of this Asian ice cream wrapped in rice dough.

MOM: The Jonas Brothers are all admit-ted mama's boys! "If you're at the venue and you happen to see our mom walk-ing around, make sure you're nice to her!" Nick offered to *Twist* in August 2008. "That's what's important to us!" Kevin added that their mom often gives thumbs-up or thumbs-down votes on potential girl-friends! In early 2008, all the Jonas guys

chipped in and bought Denise Jonas a Chopard diamond watch to thank her for all she's done!

MONROE, MARILYN: When asked by *Twist* in July 2008 which Hollywood celeb he'd love to kiss, Nick playfully offered up the blonde icon who passed away in 1962.

MOTTOS: The guys are fans of uplifting sayings. Two that have gotten them through tough times are "Stop hoping, start believ-ing!" and "You gotta pay the cost to be the boss." But their all-time favorite came from their dad: "Live like you are at the bottom even if you are at the top."

MOVIES: You know that with their sense of humor, the boys would be huge fans of funny flicks! Little brother Frankie is nick-named "Frank the Tank" in honor of Will Ferrell's character in *Old School*, and they also love the Billy Bob Thornton and Jon Heder movie, *School for Scoundrels*. For a more introspective pick, Kevin has said he loves the Hugh Grant film *About a Boy*. Joe told *J-14* in January 2008, "Girls watch action films, but they find more enter-tainment watching a love movie." He announced his own preference for kung fu movies. "Every time I leave a kung fu movie, I always get an adrenaline rush. I'm always looking around, waiting for some-body to pop out of the corner, just to make like I could punch them out." Aside from kung fu flicks, Joe also said fast-paced movies like *Rat Race*, *Casino Royale*, and the *Bourne* series were preferred viewing among the Jonases!

MYSPACE: The Jonas Brothers are among the earliest fans of using MySpace to gain and communicate with fans! In *Twist*'s May/June 2006 issue, Joe said, "Our fans are awesome. They're more like our friends. We start recognizing people, too, especially on our MySpace." Nick confirmed that "we do our own page and update on the road with our Sidekicks. We're always doing it!" In *Popstar!* in January 2007, Joe said 75 percent of their fans came from MySpace. Nick had a good theory about why that was, saying, "When we were going on our Veronicas tour, we went to their MySpace and added a bunch of their friends so people would know about us!" But beware—the guys do *not* have personal MySpaces and do *not* chat with fans online. In *CosmoGIRL!* in Summer 2008, Kevin told this story: "I encountered a girl at a meet-and-greet. She brought all these gifts and was like, 'Hi, I'm Megan. We talk online all the time.' I was like, 'Who?' She looked really concerned and said, 'I guess I was talking to someone I thought was you who wasn't.'" Nick told *Popstar!* in October 2007, "My biggest pet peeve is when people pretend to be me on MySpace. It's just, like, *annoying* when they message people as me because you never know what they're going to say."

N

NEW YORK CITY: The boys are big fans of the massive metropolis that's just a hop, skip, and a bridge away from their native Wyckoff, New Jersey! "There's always something to do—even at three in the morning!" Joe told *Twist* in September 2006. Not that Joe actually runs around Manhattan at three in the morning . . . !

NICKNAMES: Joe has been called "Danger" because he's so adventurous. "One time, I climbed twenty feet and hung onto a tower onstage. To this day I'm still wondering how that happened," he told *People*. Kevin is known as "K2" (since his dad's name is also Kevin). Nick is often called simply "Nick J." More recently, with the "Nick Jonas in 2028!" slogan, he goes by "Mr. President."

NILEY: The blended nickname for "Nick & Miley" from when they were dating! Other famous examples include Brangelina (Brad Pitt & Angelina Jolie) and Zanessa (Zac Efron & Vanessa Hudgens).

O

OBAMA, SASHA AND MALIA: In January of 2009, the Jonas Brothers visited the Obamas, their second First Family in the White House after meeting the Bushes several times for public events. They had traveled to Washington, D.C. , in order to play the Kids' Inaugural Concert, a special event for military families that also featured Miley Cyrus and Demi Lovato. While there, they attended a massive party for HuffingtonPost.com (they were mobbed and left immediately) and they also snuck into the White House to surprise Sasha and Malia Obama. The night of President Obama's inauguration, the girls were having a sleepover with some of their new friends that was topped off by a scavenger hunt designed to help them become more familiar with the White House, their new home. The final door hid the best prize of all...the JoBros were standing behind it!

OJD: "Obsessive Jonas Disorder" is a term first coined by Katie and Karleigh of jonasbrothersfan.com. It means a complete and utter devotion to all things Jonas to the point where it's hard to concentrate on anything else...you know, just being normal!

P

PARTIES: The guys love parties, and love making them special for others. They told *J-14* in August 2008 that when Nick's guitar tech Benjy offhandedly said he'd love a Jell-O Slip 'N' Slide at his birthday party, they arranged it! And for their uncle Josh, they hired a clown to make him balloon animals. Interestingly, the guys tend to have very low-key birthday parties of their own, preferring to chill with friends. Kevin's twentieth birthday consisted of a bash on their tour bus. He told *People*, "We handed out invitations to all the people working on the tour. We had pizza, ice-cream cake, cheesecake and we turned up the music.

It was really cool, but Miley couldn't come because she was grounded."

PEEPS: Ever since his effort to eat healthier (to improve his stamina on tour), Joe told *People* he's been craving Peeps, the marshmallow candies that come out every Easter.

PICKUP LINE: In *Popstar!* in September 2006, the guys offered this as their ultimate pickup line: "Are those moon pants you're wearing? 'Cause your booty's out of this *world!*"

PINKBERRY: The boys love this low-fat frozen-yogurt chain. They've been spotted there many times indulging in the healthy treat. Joe often tops it off with Fruity Pebbles.

PONE: To "pone," in Jonas slang, means to totally kick butt in a way that leaves no doubt. It comes from the gaming word "pwn" (pronounced "pawn"), which in turn came into being thanks to a common typo of the word "own." In the same way that when someone loses a game badly, people will say, "He got owned!" the Jonas Brothers will say the person got "poned" instead.

PRESIDENT: Nick Jonas has joked about running for president—he's even nicknamed "Mr. President." But could it be more than a joke? Nick told *CosmoGIRL!* in Summer 2008, "At the end of the day, why not? It would be great if in [twenty] years, I look back at this article and remember what I said. The world is a dark place right now, and I think the three of us are just trying to add some light to it."

R

RAVIOLI: One of Joe's fave Italian dishes is ravioli with meat sauce!

RINGTONE: It's not the case anymore, but did you know Nick Jonas once had one of his own songs as his ringtone? He told *Popstar!* in February 2008, "We're not ashamed to say we vote for ourselves on

Radio Disney, so to buy my ringtone? Yeah, I'll buy my ringtone."

S

SHOWER: All three JoBros sing in the shower! They told *CosmoGIRL!* their fave songs to croon are "Alison" by Elvis Costello (Nick), "Since U Been Gone" by Kelly Clarkson (Joe), and "Desperado" by the Eagles (Kevin).

STARBUCKS: Kevin is addicted! He told *Bop* in its June/July 2006 issue that Starbucks was the best part of his hometown. "Whenever my friends and I get together, we all hang out there. And when I walk in, I don't even have to order—they know what I want!" In *Tiger Beat* in December 2006, Joe reported that Kevin "has a Starbucks radar in his head. We'll be on the road, and he'll be like, 'Two miles—Starbucks!' He can smell it! And every time, he's right!"

T

TEAM HILARIO: This tongue-in-cheek side musical project featured Nick (in a mask of the Rock), Joe, Greg Garbowsky from the Jonas backup band, and their old drummer Alex Noyes. They sang "I Believe I Can Fly" at one of the Jonas Brothers' gigs in 2006. Nick was known to wear a shirt with "Team Hilario" across the chest in early 2007.

TITANIC: The boys visited "*Titanic:* The Artifact Exhibition" in Las Vegas just before one of their concerts at the urging of their tutor as part of their continuing education. The guys were given characters to play— Nick played John Jacob Astor and his mom played his wife, which cracked them both up! After the tour, Denise bought Frankie a model of the *Titanic*. The whole visit was filmed for use on their *Livin' the Dream* Disney Channel series.

TRL: The guys were obsessed with MTV's old show *Total Request Live* and getting one of their songs on its countdown. In 2006, when "Mandy" made the list, competing with the likes of videos by Madonna, they were overjoyed. "It's our dream come true!" Kevin gushed to *Tiger Beat* in its January/ February 2007 issue.

V

VACATION: In *Bop* in October 2008, Nick admitted his dream vacay would be "to the Bahamas. I love it there because they have a golf course and nice scenery."

VIDEO CHAT: Kevin's preferred method of communication is the video chat! He often indulges in this on lazy days when he doesn't have a show that night, just to catch up with pals.

W

WATSON, EMMA: Joe has told all the teen magazines that the *Harry Potter* series star is one of his all-time celebrity crushes. Do celebrities get celebrity crushes? Apparently they do! "I'll start a rumor! I have a very big crush on Emma Watson. So big! Actually, I haven't seen one of the *Harry Potter* movies. I'm going to start. She's, like, wow . . . ridiculous!" he told *Popstar!* in November 2007.

WENTZ, PETE: The guys encountered the lead singer of Fall Out Boy on his MTV series *FNMTV*. "I love Fall Out Boy's music," Nick told *m* in September 2008.

WESTLAKE: This is the Texas town where the Jonases bought a mansion—it's a short drive from where Nick was born. "It's just a place to go on vacation," Kevin told *Twist* in its October/November 2008 issue. "When we're in Texas, it doesn't feel real. I get in a golf cart, go straight to the golf course. It's the best thing ever!"

WIFFLE BALL: True fans know the brothers are obsessed with this sport—they play it every chance they get! "I like when Joe, Nick, and I play Wiffle ball inside the arenas where we have our shows," Kevin told *Twist*

in September 2008. "We'll have home run contests and smack the ball from the stage into the stands. It's a lot of fun."

WINFREY, OPRAH: The Jonas Brothers appeared on Oprah's show after their fans signed a massive petition to get them on. "She was amazing!" Joe said in *Popstar!* in August 2008. "It was just like meeting the Queen—the coolest thing ever!"

Y

YOUTUBE: The guys have *the* funniest YouTube channel ever (Youtube.com/ jonasbrothersmusic), and pioneered the idea of posting unpolished, unscripted, unedited videos on the popular site as a way to gain and entertain fans. Back in December 2006, Joe told *m*, "We love to make home movies when we're on tour. It's a good way to pass the time!" To *Popstar!* in October 2007, Kevin admitted, "YouTube is now our best friend." Instead of just passing the time, their hobby became an amazing invitation to their loyal supporters, generating 17,000,000 views for their YouTube account. The secret to their videos' success? "I know that people will want to view a video if it's hilarious," Joe told *J-14* in its October/November 2008 issue. "If it's funny, all you want to do is send it to your friends."

175

Bibliography

Bop, "A Day in the Jonas Life," June/July 2008.

_____, "Are the JoBros Crushing?" January 2008.

_____, "Be a JoBro VIP," February 2008.

_____, "Before Summer Is Over, I Have To . . ." October 2008.

_____, "*Bop's* Top 10 'Miley-isms,'" October 2007.

_____, "Boys vs. Girls: What Makes the Perfect Outdoor Date?" May 2008.

_____, "Can Girls & Guys Just Be Friends?" May 2008.

_____, "Celebrity Dreams Decoded!" December 2006.

_____, "Come to Our Studio!" September 2007.

_____, "Fact Sheet: Kevin Jonas," February 2007.

_____, "Fact Sheet: Nick Jonas," May 2007.

_____, "Have a Jonas Summer!" May 2008.

_____, "Have They Avoided a Crush?" December 2007.

_____, "I Knew I Was in Love . . ." June/July 2008.

_____, "Jonas Brothers Decoded," June/July 2007.

_____, "Jonas CD Secrets!" October 2008.

_____, "The Jonas Crushing Handbook," April 2007.

_____, "Jonas Montana?!" October 2007.

_____, "Jonas Song Secrets!" November 2007.

_____, "The Last Time I Cried . . ." May 2008.

_____, "Love on the *Camp Rock* Set?" August 2008.

_____, "Miley's Dating Drama!" February 2008.

_____, "Music News," June/July 2006.

_____, "Music News," February 2007.

_____, "My Dream Girl Is . . ." September 2008.

_____, "My Secret Journal—You Can Read It!" June/July 2007.

_____, "Real or Rumor?" May 2007.

_____, "Real or Rumor?" November 2007.

_____, "Real or Rumor?" February 2008.

_____, "Real or Rumor?" June/July 2008.

_____, "Rock Star Digs!" June/July 2006.

_____, "The Secret Lives of the Jonas Brothers," December 2007.

_____, "We Are *Burning Up!* For You!" September 2008.

_____, "We Like Girls Who . . ." December 2006.

_____, "We Would Totally Date a Fan!" April 2008.

_____, "We're All Yours!" March 2008.

_____, "Welcome to 'Jonas World,'" March 2007.

CosmoGIRL! Extra: Special Jonas Brothers Issue, Hearst, Summer 2008.

Donahue, Ann. "The Jonas Brothers Dominate a Multimedia World," *Billboard*, June 21, 2008.

Eliscu, Jenny. "Elvis Costello & The Attraction," *Rolling Stone*, October 30, 2008.

Fans' Choice: Jonas Brothers—Living the Dream!, Leisure Publishing, LLC, 2008.

Fans' Choice: Stars of Summer!, Leisure Publishing, LLC, 2008.

Fans' Choice: Triple Treat!, Leisure Publishing, LLC, 2007.

Gay, Jason. "The Clean Teen Machine," *Rolling Stone*, August 7, 2008.

J-14, "101 Weird But True Confessions," December 2007.

_____, "All Access: JoBros," October/November 2008.

_____, "Before They Were Stars," July 2006.

_____, "Behind the Scenes of the JoBros' Reality Show," July 2008.

_____, "*Camp Rock* Bonus Book," July 2008.

_____, "Catfight: The Dude Edition!" September 2008.

_____, "Celebrity Love Notes," February 2008.

_____, "Celebrity Prank War!" April 2008.

_____, "Classroom Crushes," September 2008.

_____, "Create Your Own YouTube Show!" October/November 2008.

_____, "Dating Dos & Don'ts," February 2008.

_____, "Dish with Danielle," April 2008.

_____, "Dish with Danielle," July 2008.

_____, "Dish with Danielle," August 2008.

_____, "Dish with Danielle," September 2008.

_____, "Falling for the Same Girl?" September 2008.

_____, "Friends First?" February 2008.

_____, "Guys Confess Their Deepest Secrets," April 2008.

_____, "Guys Confess Their Deepest Secrets," May/June 2008.

_____, "Hot Boys of Summer," July 2007.

_____, "How Kevin Hopes to Meet His Dream Girl," August 2008.

_____, "How to Tell if He Likes You," July 2007.

_____, "I [Heart] Snow Days," January 2008.

_____, "'I Kicked His Butt!' and Other Brotherly Stories," March 2008.

_____, "Inside Their Sweet 16s," September 2008.

_____, "Is It True?" December 2007.

_____, "Is It True?" January 2008.

_____, "Is It True?" August 2008.

_____, "Joe & Chelsea: Is It Love?" May/June 2008.

_____, "Jonas Brothers: 3-D Movie Madness," October/November 2008.

_____, "The Jonas Brothers: Easter Egg Hunks," April 2006.

_____, "The Jonas Brothers Help You Get Your Flirt On!" February 2008.

_____, "Jonas Brothers: If You Were My Girlfriend . . ." December 2007.

_____, "The Jonas Brothers: Running Themselves Ragged?" May/June 2008.

_____, "Live Like a Star!" January 2008.

_____, "Lucky in Love?" January 2008.

_____, "Miley Cyrus & the Jonas Bros: Their Biggest Fight on Tour," January 2008.

_____, "Miley Doesn't Want to Disappoint You!" August 2008.

_____, "My Parents Are So Embarrassing!" April 2008.

_____, "My Privacy Was Invaded!" August 2008.

_____, "My Very First Date," October/November 2008.

_____, "Nick Jonas: Life Without Miley," March 2008.

_____, "On a Date with the Jonas Brothers," April 2007.

_____, "Ready to Rebound?" April 2008.

_____, "Relationships Are Impossible," August 2008.

_____, "Scene Everywhere," May/June 2006.

_____, "Secrets Only a Mom Would Know," May/June 2007.

_____, "Secrets Only a Mom Would Know," May/June 2008.

_____, "Tales of Truth or Dare," July 2008.

_____, "They Called It Quits!" March 2007.

_____, "This Just In!" December 2007.

_____, "This Just In!" May/June 2008.

_____, "This Just In!" August 2008.

_____, "Touring Is Dangerous," March 2008.

_____, "The Truth About Nelena," October/November 2008.

_____, "The Unlucky Jonas Brother!" March 2008.

_____, "When I Was in High School . . ." January 2008.

_____, "Who's Hooking Up?" May/June 2008.

_____, "Yikes! Totally Embarrassing Moments," December 2007.

_____, "Your Hot List," January 2007.

Life Story: Jonas Brothers Living the Dream Summer 2008!, Bauer, Summer 2008.

Life Story: Jonas Brothers Share Every Minute of Their Incredible Rise to Fame!, Bauer, Winter 2008.

Life Story: Jonas Brothers Yearbook, Bauer, Spring 2008.

m, "Ask Us Anything!" July 2006.

_____, "Ask Us Anything!" May 2007.

_____, "Ask Us Anything!" June 2007.

_____, "Break-Ups! The Real Stories—Uncovered," March 2007.

_____, "*Camp Rock* Girls Spill JB Juice!" May 2008.

_____, "Cute Boy Confessions," January/February 2007.

_____, "Cute Boy Confessions," March 2007.

_____, "Dear *m* Girls . . . JB's *Camp Rock* Journal," December 2007.

_____, "Holiday Gift Guide," December 2006.

_____, "Hook-Ups & Heartache," October/November 2008.

_____, "JB Rumor Busters: The Real Truth!" April 2008.

_____, "JB's Love Sick on Tour!" July 2008.

_____, "Joe Tells *m*: Demi's My Guardian Angel!" July 2008.

_____, "Join JB on Tour!" December 2007.

_____, "Jonas Bros: The Last Time We Cried," January/February 2008.

_____, "Jonas Bros Reveal: Our Perfect Date," October/November 2008.

_____, "Jonas Bros Reveal: We Didn't Fit In!" August 2008.

_____, "Jonas Brothers Prank Aly & AJ," August 2006.

_____, "Jonas Rumor Patrol: Our Secret Love Promise," July 2007.

_____, "Karaoke Date with JB!" May 2008.

_____, "Love on the Set of *Camp Rock*?" June 2008.

_____, "The *m* Insider," June 2007.

_____, "The *m* Insider," March 2008.

_____, "The *m* Insider: Miley & Jonas Bonus Edition!" January/February 2008.

_____, "The *m* Insider," October/November 2008.

_____, "Miley's Shocking Confession: Nick Saved My Life," October/November 2008.

_____, "More Blog Buzz!" July 2006.

_____, "Rule Your School," September 2008.

_____, "Spend the Day with JB!" October/November 2008.

_____, "Star Scrapbook," July 2007.

_____, "Star Scrapbook," July 2008.

_____, "Star Scrapbook," August 2008.

_____, "Star Scrapbook," September 2008.

_____, "Truth or Rumor?" January/February 2008.

_____, "Truth or Rumor?" May 2008.

_____, "Truth or Rumor?" October/November 2008.

_____, "Truth or Rumor? Special," May 2007.

_____, "The Untold Story Behind . . . Nick & Miley's Love," December 2007.

_____, "We Survived a Class Catastrophe!" September 2008.

_____, "We're Searching For Summer Love!" June 2008.

_____, "What Makes a Great Kiss?" March 2008.

_____, "What's Their Summer Smooch Secret?" July 2008.

_____, "Who's Making JB Blush?" March 2008.

People Special Collector's Edition: All About the Jonas Brothers, June 2008.

Pixie, "Welcome to *Camp Rock*!" Summer 2008.

Popstar!, "3 Jonas Brothers, a Photo Shoot and *Popstar!*" November 2007.

_____, "Batter Up!" April 2008.

_____, "The Best & Worst Celebrity Pickup Lines," September 2006.

_____, "Break-Out Stars of 2006!" January 2006.

_____, "Dream Themes!" April 2007.

_____, "Eyewitness," July 2008.

_____, "Eyewitness," August 2008.

_____, "Get into Nick's Head!" January 2008.

_____, "Happy Campers *Camp Rock* Mini-Mag!" July 2008.

_____, "Idol Intros!" January 2007.

_____, "JoBros Invade *Hannah Montana*: All the Facts!" September 2007.

_____, "JoBros on the Go!" January 2008.

_____, "Jonas @ Honor Society's Gig!" November 2008.

_____, "Jonas Brothers' Crush Cues!" July 2007.

_____, "Jonas Brothers Family Firsts!" September 2006.

_____, "Jonas Brothers 'Live' Mini-Mag!" May 2008.

_____, "Jonas in Paradise!" August 2007.

_____, "Jonas Lessons!" March 2007.

_____, "Jonas Brothers Timeline!" December 2008.

_____, "Jonas Tour: Top Secrets!" July 2008.

_____, "Musical Notes!" August 2006.

_____, "MySpace MyThbusters!" October 2007.

_____, "Nick J on Broadway!" May 2008.

_____, "Niley—No More? The Real Deal!" April 2008.

_____, "People Wanna Know!" August 2006.

_____, "People Wanna Know!" June 2007.

_____, "People Wanna Know!" August 2007.

_____, "People Wanna Know!" January 2008.

_____, "People Wanna Know!" April 2008.

_____, "People Wanna Know!" May 2008.

_____, "People Wanna Know!" July 2008.

_____, "People Wanna Know!" December 2008.

_____, "The Perks (and Quirks) of Being a Jonas!" October 2007.

_____, "Play Their Music: On the Road with the Jonas Brothers!" October 2008.

_____, "Quick Nick Picks!" March 2008.

_____, "Rude & Embarrassing!" October 2006.

_____, "Rude & Embarrassing!" June 2007.

_____, "Rude & Embarrassing!" January 2008.

_____, "Rude & Embarrassing!" February 2008.

_____, "The 6th Annual _Popstar!_ Poptastic Awards!" August 2007.

_____, "Summer Blockbusters: Jonas Brothers," July 2006.

_____, "TV Talk," March 2008.

_____, "Ultimate DC Games Mini-Mag!" August 2008.

_____, "The United States of Jonas Mini-Mag!" November 2008.

_____, "Where in the World Is . . . JB?" August 2008.

Rosenberg, Carissa. "Miley: You Think You Know Her—But You Don't,"
Seventeen, September 2008.

Smith, Ethan. "How Disney Is Reviving a Band Still in Its Teens," _Wall Street
Journal_, July 19, 2007.

Teen, "Boys of Summer," Summer 2008.
_____, "Grab Breakfast with the Jonas Brothers," Winter 2008.

Tiger Beat, "5 Questions for . . . Kevin Jonas," May 2007.

_____, "5 Questions for . . . Nick Jonas," August 2007.

_____, "100 Star Secrets!" November 2007.

_____, "All-Access Jonas!" July 2008.

_____, "April Fools," May 2008.

_____, "_Camp Rock_ Crush!" May 2008.

_____, "Can I Have Your Autograph?" November 2007.

_____, "The Craziest Thing I've Done for Love . . ." June 2007.

_____, "The Fan I'll Never Forget!" September 2008.

_____, "Hollywood Hot Spot," October 2007.

_____, "Hollywood Hot Spot," January/February 2008.

_____, "Hollywood Hot Spot," May 2008.

_____, "I Was Lonely," September 2008.

_____, "I Would Date a Fan If . . ." March 2007.

_____, "Is Nick Ready For Love?" August 2008.

_____, "Is There a Jonas Jealousy?" August 2008.

_____, "JoBro Rumor 411," March 2008.

_____, "The JoBros Get Personal!" June 2008.

_____, "Jonas Beat," March 2008.

_____, "Jonas Beat," June 2008.

_____, "Jonas Beat," September 2008.

_____, "Jonas Flip for You!" August 2008.

_____, "Jonas vs. Jonas," September 2008.

_____, "Meet the Jonas Brothers!" July 2006.

_____, "My Brothers Drive Me Crazy!" December 2006.

_____, "My Fans Rule!" June 2007.

_____, "My JoBro Crush Is . . ." January/February 2008.

_____, "Nick's Stage Secret," December 2007.

_____, "OMG I Was Sooooo Embarrassed!" September 2008.

_____, "Party Like a Star!" December 2006.

_____, "Seeing Stars," October 2008.

_____, "Shhh . . . I Have a Secret!" April 2007.

_____, "Shhh . . . I Have a Secret!" September 2007.

_____, "Summer Camp Scoop!" July 2008.

_____, "Summer Fun—Hollywood Style," July 2006.

_____, "They Did What for Love?" November 2006.

_____, "*Tiger Beat* Presents: The Jonas Brothers Mini-Mag," July 2007.

_____, "*Tiger Beat's* 150 Best Things About 2006!" January/February 2007.

_____, "The Top 8," August 2008.

_____, "The Top 8," October 2008.

_____, "We Love You, Too!" June 2007.

_____, "We Thought We Were Going to Die!" September 2007.

_____, "You Love the Jonas Brothers Because . . ." March 2008.

Tiger Beat Celebrity Spectacular!, "10 Things You Didn't Know About the JoBros," Fall 2008.

_____, "Chatting with Kevin!" Summer 2008.

_____, "Jonas Pop Quiz!" Fall 2008.

_____, "Jonas Rumor Control," Summer 2008.

_____, "Jonas Shoot Secrets!" Summer 2008.

_____, "Jonesin' for Joe!" Summer 2008.

_____, "Meet the Real-Life Jonas Sister!" Summer 2008.

_____, "Nuts About Nick!" Summer 2008.

_____, "The Secret Lives of the Jonas Brothers," Fall 2008.

_____, "Your Jonas Backstage Pass!" Summer 2008.

Twist, "Breakup Feuds!" May/June 2008.

_____, "*Camp Rock* Diaries," July 2008.

_____, "Chemistry on the Set of *Camp Rock*!" May/June 2008.

_____, "Cody Reveals: Why Guys Don't Like to Dance!" August 2008.

_____, "Collectible *Camp Rock* Booklet!" April 2008.

_____, "Couple Update," January 2007.

_____, "The Craziest Thing I Did for a Guy," May/June 2007.

_____, "Eat Breakfast with JB," April 2008.

_____, "Fact or Fiction?" February 2008.

_____, "Fact or Fiction?" April 2008.

_____, "Fact or Fiction?" May/June 2008.

_____, "Flashback: Jonas Brothers," October/November 2006.

_____, "For the Record," October/November 2006.

_____, "For the Record," February 2007.

_____, "Girl Bands vs. Boy Bands," February 2006.

_____, "Hallway Hookups!" September 2008.

_____, "Hanging with the Jonas Brothers," September 2006.

_____, "Hot Stuff," May/June 2006.

_____, "I Don't Understand Why Girls . . ." February 2008.

_____, "JB's Biggest Month Ever!" September 2008.

_____, "JB's Stage Secrets," January 2008.

_____, "JB Changed Our Lives," February 2008.

_____, "JB: The Dates We'll Never Forget!" May/June 2008.

_____, "JB Hangs with Fans at the DC Games," July 2008.

_____, "JB Reveals: The Secret Side We Hide!" September 2008.

_____, "JB: We Get Shy Around Girls!" March 2008.

_____, "JB: We're Dating Again!" August 2008.

_____, "JB: We're Looking for Love!" April 2008.

_____, "Jonas: We Fight Over Girls!" July 2008.

_____, "Kissing Catastrophes," May/June 2006.

_____, "Livin' the Dream!" May/June 2008.

_____, "Looks Boys Love," April 2007.

_____, "Lucky Stars," March 2007.

_____, "Miley & Nick: Getting Close on Tour," December 2007.

_____, "Miley & Nick's Holiday on Tour," January 2008.

_____, "Miley Dishes on Dating Nick," February 2008.

_____, "My Perfect Girl," March 2007.

_____, "The New Girls in JB's Life," January 2008.

_____, "Nick and Joe Shop on Tour!" May/June 2008.

_____, "Nick Opens Up!" February 2008.

_____, "Nick Tells All at *Twist*'s Photo Shoot!" March 2008.

_____, "Nick's Scariest Moment: I Thought I Was Going to Die!" July 2007.

_____, "Our Biggest Prank War!" October/November 2008.

_____, "Our Secret Weapon: Texting Our Crushes," December 2007.

_____, "Rumor Patrol," May/June 2007.

_____, "Rumor Patrol," January 2008.

_____, "Rumor Patrol," April 2008.

_____, "Rumor Patrol: Couple Edition," July 2008.

_____, "Shout Outs," October/November 2006.

_____, "Sibling Rivalry," July 2006.

_____, "Spring Fever," April 2008.

_____, "Stargazing," December 2007.

_____, "Stars Answer Your Love Questions," February 2008.

_____, "Stars Answer Your Love Questions," March 2008.

_____, "Stars Answer Your Love Questions," April 2008.

_____, "Summer Love Secrets," July 2007.

_____, "Summer Tour Secrets," May/June 2006.

_____, "Trick-or-Treat Kiss & Tells," October/November 2008.

_____, "The Truth About Niley!" March 2008.

_____, "*Twist* Joins JB in DC!" October/November 2008.

_____, "What's in *Twist*!" August 2008.

_____, "What's in *Twist*!" September 2008.

_____, "Who's Flirting Backstage?" August 2008.

_____, "Winter Wishes: Secret Kisses," January 2008.

_____, "Your Chance to Hang with JB!" July 2008.

OFFICIAL JONAS BROTHERS SITES!

myspace.com/jonasbrothers

jonasbrothers.com

OTHER SITES!

jonasbrothersfan.com

myspace.com/popstarmagazine

oceanupped.wordpress.com

popstaronline.com

tigerbeatmag.com